SELEC NAT NOTES

By

Alan Ashpool

In his book the author has selected for publication a number of the 'Nature Notes' that he has written over the years for his local church magazine. A number of the illustrations in the original articles have been replaced with more fitting ones.

For Doreen

Without her help I would never have
written these Nature Notes

First published March 2010 by Alan Ashpool,
Trumps In Cottage, Whitchurch Canonicorum,
Bridport, Dorset, DT6 6RH.

Printed and bound in Great Britain
by Catford Print Centre
3, Bellingham Road
Catford, London, SE6 2PN

AUTHOR'S FOREWORD

Our Parish Magazine is published every month and covers the whole of the Marshwood Vale in West Dorset. It mainly deals with church matters but villagers can get articles or information published in it about any subject. When insufficient copy was coming forward the Editor actively sought articles for inclusion. At that time there was quite a lot being written about the effects of global warming so I decided to write an article for the magazine about its possible effects on local flora and fauna. It pointed out how certain wild flowers, insects and amphibians were appearing earlier and earlier each year and suggested that this might be due to global warming. I did not see myself as a naturalist but rather as a nature lover who wanted to bring the joys of watching our wildlife to as many people as possible, so I made the article as simple as possible leaving out any technical or scientific facts, and illustrated it with a picture of red admiral butterflies sipping nectar from wildflowers. For want of a better title I called it 'Nature Notes' and it was accepted and duly published in the magazine. It was warmly received and several people phoned me and asked whether I could write any more articles. So 'Nature Notes' was born!

For the first couple of years I wrote an article every two months. The subject varied greatly but there was a standard layout on an A5 page with several illustrations down the left-hand side. Again they were warmly received by readers and I came under pressure to write an article on a regular monthly basis. Finding completely different subjects each month, and also illustrations about those subjects, entailed a lot of research on my part but I also learnt a great deal about nature that had passed me by earlier. These discoveries included fiction, poetry, music and folklore about nature. There were sayings about the weather, the time of year and church festivals, as well as more down to earth matters such as what food to eat, and trees to plant, or how birds and butterflies might be attracted to the garden. I also found out about the need for action to preserve the many species that are under threat because of the way we farm, hunt, fish or cut down trees for timber. This need for action also encompassed global warming, a subject I often returned to, which was seen as the greatest threat to many species. There were a few local success stories however. In Dorset these included a campaign to save the water vole from disappearing completely and another to keep track of a decreasing number of brown hares.

I continue to get people contacting me about various aspects of subjects raised in Nature Notes. In some cases I can help right away, but if not I try to find an answer by further research. The learning process continues! Recently I became involved in The Living Churchyards Project. This was set up by the Dorset Wildlife Trust to encourage wildlife in many of Dorset's old churchyards and our wonderful churchyard of St. Candida and Holy Cross has been accepted as the Best Newcomer to the Project.

For this collection of Nature Notes I have used new illustrations based mainly on the nature photographs that I have produced over many years.

Alan Ashpool, Trumps In Cottage, Whitchurch Canonicorum

A Selection of Nature Notes Published in 1999

May

The wild flowers that grow in and around Whitchurch seem to make their first appearance earlier and earlier each year. *Snowdrops* at the beginning of January and *Primroses* not much later. The wonderful *Lesser Celandine* and *Colt's-foot* in mid February. *Greater Stichwort, Lungwort* and *Lady's Smock* in early March. Is this because 'Global Warming' has already started in earnest?

Certainly the Winters have got milder over the past few years. *Frogs* and *Toads* have started spawning about one month earlier than before. Clumps of frog's spawn were deposited in my small garden pond in early January. *Toads* need larger ponds in which to breed so the water does not warm up as quickly as in smaller ones. Nevertheless the long strings of toad's spawn were visible in some large farm ponds as early as the end of February. Another sign of an early spring was the appearance of *Brimstone, Peacock* and *Small Tortoiseshell* butterflies in my garden in the first week of March. These had probably been insects that had hibernated over the winter rather than newly emerged specimens. Again they would not normally be seen until the end of the month.

If this trend continues perhaps we will see flora and fauna in May which do not normally appear until June or even later. Perhaps for instance *Foxglove, Ox-eye Daisy* and *Birds-foot Trefoil* will be in full flower at the beginning of May. *Dragonflies* and *Burnet Moths* could be on the wing at the same time, *Red Admiral* and *Painted Lady Butterflies* might also make an appearance. It is also possible that some species who are normally native to warmer climes may pay a visit. Readers of this Magazine may like to watch out for them.

Lady's Smock

July

There seems to have been a greater number of *Song Thrushes* involved in nest building activities this year. In the Fifties the *Song Thrush* was one of our commonest birds. Sadly numbers have fallen dramatically since then and today it is almost an endangered species. Perhaps the corner has now been turned this year and we can hopefully look forward to an increase in the numbers of this wonderful bird.

The early cutting of the lane verges in and around Whitchurch has quite rightly aroused an outcry amongst residents. Not only will the number of wild flowers be affected in future years but it will also effect other wild life. The larvae of the *Orange Tip* butterfly uses *Garlic Mustard* for its food plant in this area, a plant which mainly thrives in lane verges. Even the normal cutting in Mid-June results in a reduction of the numbers of this splendid Spring butterfly in the following year. Many of our native song birds have a third brood in June and the noise of cutting the lane verges can result in deserted nests. Obviously parts of the lane verges need to be cut back for road safety reasons but perhaps this could be more selective in future and, if possible, not until the end of June.

Wild Flowers on a Lane Verge

October

Early Autumn is the time to look for wild mushrooms. These make good subjects for   artists, potters and photographers. Some scientists now think that fungi are closer to the Animal Kingdom than to the Plant Kingdom. All in all they are fascinating organisms and well worth the time seeking them out. If they are to be collected for culinary purposes however it is important that they are correctly identified. It is suggested that the advice of an expert on the subject should be used, or a very good book on fungi should be consulted, so that they can be correctly identified. In this way any deadly ones can be avoided. A number of good edible specimens which are easily identified occur in this area.

.   The commonest include *the Parasol, Giant Puffball, Shaggy Inkcap, Blewit, Oyster Mushroom* and the *Eared Mushroom* together with the *Common Field and Horse Mushrooms.* All of these make good eating. Only young specimens should be picked and only enough for your own use. The *Parasol Mushroom* occurs in meadows and is one of the first to appear. Use the cap only and this should be sliced and cooked in garlic butter. It is a very meaty mushroom which goes well with scrambled eggs. *Giant Puffballs* are often found in hedgerows and are best cut into thick slices dipped in egg and breadcrumbs and then fried. *Shaggy Inkcaps* which often occur on waste ground are very delicate and best cooked in a soufflé. Only unopened specimens should be used. *Blewits* often occur in orchards and are best fried in oil for breakfast. *Oyster Mushrooms* can be found on old tree stumps and are very good in stir fry recipes. *Eared*

Mushrooms occur on old elder trees and are very like the Cloud Mushrooms used in Chinese and Thai cooking. *Common Field and Horse Mushrooms* are found in meadows and are used like the mushrooms bought in a shop. Their flavour is much better however.

A Parasol Mushroom

December

As the Winter Solstice approaches now is the time to start feeding our garden birds. This will repay them for keeping the numbers of insect pests down during Spring and Summer as well as for singing to us during that period. Each species likes a different kind of food so the more varied a menu you can offer the more kinds of birds you will be helping. Peanuts, mixed bird seed, suet, apples, mealworms(bought as angling bait), bread, and meat scraps are all acceptable as well as baked potatoes. Try hanging out the bones of the Sunday joint! All this food should be placed fairly high well out of reach of the local cats. If you have a bird table it is also helpful to put out a dish of warm water when the weather is frosty. In my garden the following birds have been seen feeding on the food that we have provided:-

Blue Tits	*Coal Tits*
Willow Tits	*Song Thrushes*
Fieldfares	*House Sparrows*
Green finches	*Nuthatches*
Tree Creepers	*Pied Wagtails*
Hedge Sparrows	*Goldcrests*
Starlings	*Great Tits*
Long- tailed Tits	*Blackbirds*
Mistle Thrushes	*Redwings*
Chaffinches	*Gold finches*
Green Woodpeckers	*Robins*
Grey Wagtails	*Wrens*

What a joy it has been to watch these creatures accepting this food and knowing that we are helping them survive the Winter.

A Nuthatch

A Selection of Nature Notes Published in 2000

February

Now that the days are getting longer gardeners might wish to consider setting aside part of their land as a *'Nature Garden'*. Such an area will attract a wide variety of wildlife and help some of the more hard pressed species to survive. The flowers of the plants and shrubs listed below will attract many varieties of butterflies. They will also provide nectar for bees. Most of them can be grown from seed or struck as cuttings. Chiltern Seeds of Ulverston can supply seeds for all of them

Agastache, Agrostemma, Bergamot, Buddleia, Catmint, Candytuft, Cornflower, Corn-marigold, Echinops, Fleabane, Honesty, Hebe, Knap-weed, Night Scented Stock, Ox-eye Daisy, Primulas, Purple Loosestriff, Red Valerian, Sweet William, Siberian Wallflower,Teasel, Tithonia and *Vipers Burgloss*.

Other shrubs can be grown that will provide berries for birds in Autumn and Winter e.g. *Pyracanthas, Cotoneasters, Berberis, Viburnums, Rowan etc.*

A small pond will provide a breeding site for *Frogs, Newts* and *Dragonflies*. This could be made either by using a pre-formed rigid plastic container or by lining a dug out shape with rubber/plastic sheeting. Wild flowers such as *Yellow Flag Irises* can be planted in and around the margins to provide shelter for the pond's inhabitants.

. If there are suitable trees nesting boxes can be put up to provide additional accommodation for some of the birds in the garden. A number of different models are available for *Tits, Robins, Nuthatches,*

Treecreepers, and *Flycatchers.* Details of these can be found in Nature Magazines.

A Painted Lady Butterfly on Buddleia

April

April is the month when most of our visiting Summer birds arrive. A few early ones will have arrived in March and a few will leave it until May but, by and large, April is the month. The insects on which many of these visitors, and their young, depend for food become abundant as temperatures warm up. Many plants and bushes start breaking out into leaf and provide cover for nests. Spring and Summer would not seem the same without these lovely creatures with their wonderful songs and aerial aerobatics! What a joy!

Visiting birds which might be seen or heard in this area include:-
Swallows, Swifts, House Martins, Chiffchaffs, Willow Warblers, Spotted Flycatchers, Turtle Doves, Cuckoos and Garden Warblers,
April is also the month when early butterflies are on the wing. Some species will have hibernated during the colder months as mature insects. Others will have spent the Winter in the chrysalis stage. It is a sure sign that Spring has arrived when you see these beautiful creatures searching for nectar from the flowers of such plants as Aubretia and Honesty.

Butterflies which might be seen in this area during April include:-
Comma, Peacock, Small Tortoishell, Greenveined White, Brimstone, Orangetip, Holly Blue, and Speckled Wood

Enjoyable hearing and seeing!

A Brimstone Butterfly

June

The flush of Spring wild flowers is now almost over and will be followed by the early Summer varieties. A number of these will appear locally in June, especially by the side of streams and in the lane verges which have been set aside as wild flower areas by the District Council. We are lucky to have so many of these in and around Whitchurch. Look out for the following:-

Wild Rose, Yellow Iris, Blue Bugle, Common Mallow,   Convolvulus,Foxgloves, Herb   Robert, Honeysuckle, Marsh Marigold, Ox-eye Daisy, Ragged Robin,and Red Campion.

June is the month when a number of *Dragonflies* start mating and egg laying. British *Dragonflies* are divided into two groups which are based on their flight habits. There are *Hawkers* which have a strong sustained flight and *Darters* who tend to 'dart' out of the waterside plants and then return to their resting place. Look out for these beautiful creatures along the banks of streams and of ponds.

Quite a number of butterflies are on the wing in this area in June including:-

Green Hairstreaks, Large Skippers, Meadow Browns, Painted Ladies, Red Admirals, Ringlets, Small Pearl Bordered Fritillaries and Wood Whites.

The last two are very rare. For a number of years a local colony of *Small Pearl Bordered Fritillaries* has existed on the South side of Hardown Hill and appears to be hanging on. Last year I was informed that a small number of *Wood Whites* had been seen in a newly cleared area of Prime Coppice. Up to then only two colonies of these small delicately marked whites were known to have existed in the whole of Dorset .

A Newly Hatched Dragonfly

September

September and October are the months of *Nature's Bounty*. The hedgerows, fields and woods are full of fruits, nuts and fungi. All of these provide easy food for animals and birds before the lean Winter months. Providing we do not harvest too many of them they can also be used by us to make cheap delicious food and drink.

The fruits to be seen in this area which might tempt readers include *Blackberries, Sloes, Elderberries, Rose-hips, Rowan berries, Crab apples* and *Hawthorn berries.* There are many recipes for using these fruits as food or for making wine. These are often given in books about countryside cooking and wine-making. One I read recently gave recipes for *Blackberry Pudding, Blackberry Tremble, Sloe and Apple Jelly, Elderberry Rob, Elderberry Sauce, Rose Hip and Honey Syrup, Rowan Jelly, Crab Apple Cake, Crab Apple and Date Wine, and Hawthorn Berry Wine* to name but a few.

There are a number of superstitions about picking wild fruits. For instance local people will probably refrain from picking Blackberries after Old Michaelmas Day — 11th October because it is unlucky after that date. The tradition arose because the devil was apparently thrown out of heaven on that day and, not being happy when he landed in a blackberry bush, he cursed it. On the anniversary of his downfall he breathes all over the fruits, and anyone who gathers them will have bad luck.

The commonest nut in this area is probably the Hazelnut. The only problem is that it is only really good when fully ripe and, if left to then, the squirrels and jays will get there first. If enough ripe nuts are found however, they can be used to make a very rich cake or buttered tart.

In October 1999 I gave details in this Magazine of the wild mushrooms to be found in The Marshwood Vale together with suggestions as to how they might be used. Now is the time to start looking for them.   Good Hunting!

Hazelnuts

November

Now that their leaves have fallen this is a good time to look at the silhouettes of our wonderful native deciduous trees. Each one has a distinctive outline.

In the Marshwood Vale the magnificent *Oak* predominates. It is broad and stocky. How well it has served us over the years. Not for nothing is it sometimes referred to as the King of trees. There are also a large number of *Ash, Beech* and *Sycamores*. The *Ash* which is said to have been named after the colour of its bark, is tall and slender. Its branches more evenly spaced than those of the Oak. The branches of the *Beech* are also evenly spaced and soar to a great height. When their leaves fall they retain their brilliant colouring for a long time which contrasts brilliantly with the smooth grey bark. The *Beech* is a painters tree and often features in Autumn landscapes. The branches of the *Sycamore* are also fairly evenly spaced. The trunk is grey and a little scaly. Some authorities say that the true name of this tree is the *Great Maple*. In smaller numbers other large trees to be seen locally include the *Horse Chestnut, Willow* and several *Poplars*. See how many you can identify without having their leaves to refer to!

There is a certain amount of Folklore about trees. For instance it is said that if in the Spring the *Ash* is in full leaf before the *Oak* we shall have a rainy Summer. If however the *Oak* is out first then the Summer will be fine. It is also said that the Willow is a symbol of grief for those who have been forsaken in love.

Oak Trees in Winter

> # A Selection of Nature Notes Published in 2001

January

As far as the weather is concerned January is an unpredictable month. Sometimes there are very low temperatures, heavy frosts and a lot of snow. On the other hand there may be periods of quite warm weather. There are many sayings about this fickle month, One that I like is *'Winter weather and womens' thoughts often change'*.

In a mild month a number of things will happen which are normally associated with February. *Foxes* will seek mates. *Moles* will be busy making molehills. These freshly dug piles of earth are very important to many birds who search them for insects and other food. *Rooks* will visit their old rookeries to decide whether or not it is getting near nesting time. These meetings are sometimes referred to as *Rook Parliaments.* Wild flowers which might be early include *Snowdrops, Red Dead Nettle* and the odd stray *Primrose, Coltsfoot* and *Violet.* Catkins on *Hazel* will appear at the beginning of the month including the small red female tassels.

Butterflies will not be seen on the wing but a few might be noticed stirring in the corners of warm buildings where they have been hibernating. Look out for *Peacocks, Red Admirals* and *Small Tortoiseshells.*

In any January many birds go around in flocks. What wonderful collective nouns are used for these groups e.g. *A Charm of Goldfinches, A Clamour of Rooks, A Murmation of Starlings!* How many more do you know?

Snowdrops

February

February can be even more fickle than January as far as the weather is concerned. On some days the temperature can soar to the higher teens Centigrade but on others it can fall to well below freezing with snow and frost. These extremes can have a great effect on our fauna and flora.

Warm days can lead to the early appearance of some of our most magnificent butterflies such as the *Peacock*. *Small Tortoieshell* and *Brimstone*. A number of *Bees* and *Hoverflies* may also venture out. *Frogs* will leave their Winter quarters and look for ponds in which to deposit their spawn. Early nesting birds such as the *Mistle Thrush* will start building nests and may even lay eggs. Some wild flowers normally associated with later months will come into bloom e.g. the beautiful *Lesser Celandine.*

In severe weather however, things are very different. The frozen ground makes it very difficult for birds to find food such as earthworms. Ice on ponds make it impossible for frogs to start spawning. Butterflies remain in hibernation. Early wild flowers are cut back by the frost. We can help the birds when temperatures fall by putting out food, but there is not much else we can do other than sit tight and wait for things to improve.

There are a lot of sayings about the weather in February. One that I particularly like, and which might have an element of truth in it, is:-

'If Candlemas Day be fair and bright Winter will have a further flight,
But if Candlemas Day be clouds and rain, Winter is gone and will not come again'

Lesser Celandine

March

   In March *Spring* really does get under way. This time of year the fauna and flora that are seen have always been an inspiration to many of the English poets. Most readers will be familiar with William Wordsworth and his host of golden daffodils. In Dorset *Spring* had a great influence on William Barnes who wrote many poems about the Seasons in the wonderful local dialect. The following verses are taken from one of his poems called The Spring:

WHEN wintry weather's all a-done,
An' brooks do sparkle in the run,
An' ralisy-buildèn rooks do vlee
Wi' sticks toward their elem tree;
When birds do zing, an' we can zee
Upon the boughs the buds o' spring,
Then I'm as happy as a king,
A-yield wi' health an' zunsheen.

Vor then the cowslip's hangèn flow'r
A-wetted in the zunny show'r,
Do grow wi' vi'lets, sweet o' smell,
Bezide the wobd-screen'd grgle's bell;
Where drushes' aggs, wi' sky-blue shell Do lie in mossy nest among
The thorns, while they do zing their zong
At evenèn in the zunsheen.

Sadly the Song Thrush is not as common as it was in his time. Several theories have been put forward as to why this is. Some people say it is because of the increase in the number of Magpies who plunder nests. Others say it is because of slug pellets. Violets also are not as plentiful which has been put down to a lack of coppicing. This in turn has led to a big decrease in the number of Fritillary butterflies who use Violets as a foodplant for their offspring. Happily there are still plenty of Cowslips to be seen with their wonderful bells.

Cowslip Bells

April

In April more and more birds take up nest building. What a variety of designs they use. Some birds such as *Lapwings* use a simple scrape in the ground for incubating their eggs. Others such as the majority of *Tits* use an existing hole in a tree trunk in which to build their nest. others such as *Green Woodpeckers* dig out their own hole. Birds such as *Rooks* and *Crows* create a very large nest out of twigs. Some smaller birds such as *Chaffinches* and *Long Tailed Tits* build soft intricate nests out of moss, lichens and down. Each species of bird seems to have its own individual style of nest building. Two separate species are unlikely to build identical nests. How does an individual bird know what kind of nest to build. Some say it is pure instinct, others have more fanciful ideas. I do not know why but I rather like the idea expressed in the following lines by Lord Grey of Falloden:

With nests, as with plumage, we find
differences so great that they seem to be manifesting Nature's love of infinite variety.

Eggs have been used for centuries as a symbol of Spring which was a time of germination and fertilization. People exchanged coloured eggs during their Spring celebrations. When I was evacuated to Lancaster during the War we painted eggs, if we could get them, and rolled them down slopes in the local park. This was called *pace egging* and was said to symbolize the rolling away of the stone from Christ's tomb.

A Lapwing's Nest

May

If movement restrictions are still in place in May to help stop the spread of the terrible Foot and Mouth Disease, we must do all we can by limiting our nature excursions to our gardens and roadside verges.

The month is a very busy one for our *Fauna* and *Flora*. .Wild flowers to be seen include *Blue Bells, Cow Parsley, Cowslips, Greater Stitchwort, Lady's Smock* and *Red Campion*. A number of trees and shrubs are also in flower. Some such as the *Horse Chestnut* have a show of spectacular candelabra. Others such as the Lime are more modest The most profuse blossoms to be seen at this time are on the *Hawthorn*. This is often been referred to as *May Blossom* and many things have been written about it. One of my favourites is

' When the May blossom too early shows.
We will have still many snows.'

Many butterflies will be on the wing during May a lot of them in gardens and along roadside hedgerows. Look out for the following:- *Brimstone, Comma, Green-veined White, Holly Blue, Orange Tip, Peacock, Small Copper, Small Tortoiseshell, Speckled Wood* and *Wall* What a joy it is to watch these creatures!

Another delight at this time of the year is hearing the birds singing the dawn chorus. It is generally thought that birds sing to mark out their territory but some people think that they also sing for the sheer joy of it. The *Blackbird* is usually the first to break into song about 40 minutes before sunrise. It is closely followed by the *Song Thrush, Robin, Mistle Thrush, Turtle Dove, Willow Warbler* and *Wren*. Size of bird seems to have little bearing on the loudness of the song. In fact the tiny Wren possibly has the loudest voice of the lot. Happy listening!

May Blossom

June

June is a busy month for insects especially bees. They are very important creatures because as they collect nectar they pollinate our flowers, fruit and vegetable plants Where would we be without them?

In addition to the well known Honey-bee there are also a number of different kinds of *Bumble-bees, Cuckoo Bees* and *Solitary Bees*. Honey-bees and Bumble-bees live in colonies the nests of the later are usually smaller constructions than the well known bee-hive. *Cuckoo Bees* make no nest of their own but take over Bumblebee colonies where they kill the queen and have their young raised by the host workers. The Solitary Bees form the greatest number of species of Bees in this country. They make small nests where the female lays a few eggs before she moves on to other nests. In each nest she leaves a store of food to see her offspring through the Winter. When all her eggs have been laid she dies.

There are a number of sayings about Bees especially Honey-bees. The most well known is probably:

'*A swarm of bees in June
is worth a silver spoon*.'

. A number of our native lizards may be seen sunning themselves on warm June days. In this area I have seen both *Common Lizards* and *Slow-worms* basking in the sun. Although the later is legless and looks more like a snake it really is a lizard.. Both feed mainly on earthworms and are harmless creatures. Sometimes these lizards can be seen with part of their tail missing. This is often the result of a predator catching them by the end of the tail and the lizard escaping by breaking off the end of it. These stumps eventually regrow into a new tail but it is never as slender and long as the original one.

I have never seen the rarer *Sand-lizard* in this area. In Dorset it is said to be restricted to the New Forest.

A Honey Bee Collecting Nectar

July

July is said to take its name from Julius Caesar. It is often the hottest month of the year but it can be wet. There are several country sayings about the weather in July. One that I like is:-

' *I f the first of July be rainy weather*
It will rain for full four weeks together'

There is also the well known superstition about St Swithen's Day.

The month is a very busy one for butterflies and other insects. Where would we be without the sight and sounds of these creatures? The butterflies that are most associated with the Summer and the countryside are probably those belonging to what is known as the *'Brown family'*. Nearly all of them can be seen flying in meadows and along hedgerows in this area during July. Look out for the following, which are listed in roughly their order of appearance:- *Speckled Wood, Marbled White, Ringlet, Meadow Brown, Small Heath, Gatekeeper, Grayling* and *Wall*. The caterpillars of these lovely creatures feed on varieties of native grasses, they are especially prolific on meadows that are not cut too early.

July is also a good month to watch and listen to *Grasshoppers*. These harmless creatures have the ability to leap great distances and also to sing.

The singing sounds are produced by a process called stridulation. On the inner surface of the male grasshopper's large thigh joint there is a row of pegs. Hard ridges are found on the insect's forewings. When the legs are moved over the wings these vibrate giving rise to the sound. Each species produces a different song due to a variation in the number of pegs. Grasshoppers use their songs mainly during the breeding season and to indicate territorial boundaries.

Most birds will stop singing in July once they have fledged their young and no longer need to proclaim their territorial boundaries. The wonderful Blackbird is one of the last to be heard and sadly, for us, will not be heard again until next Spring.

A Young Blackbird

September

In early September the sea around our coasts is at its warmest. It is a good time to look at the marine life that flourishes in the rock pools that are on our local beaches. When the tide recedes these areas shelter sea animals from the hostile environment of the open shore.

Fish that live in rock pools include *Shanny, Corkwing, Wrasse, Butterfish,* various *Gobies* and *Blennies.* The *Shanny* is probably the most common. It is the rock pool dweller that children on Summer seaside holidays spend hours trying to catch in a net, in a bucket or even with their bare hands. Does this bring back memories?

Other common inhabitants of these pools include crabs and prawns. The commonest crab is the *Shore Crab.* This creature adjusts to growth by shedding its old hard shell to show the soft replacement that has been developing underneath. The discarded shells are a common sight on beaches. Female crabs are often seen carrying a mass of eggs under a broad abdomen flap. The males have a narrower abdomen. Sometimes the males appear to be carrying eggs but in fact these are parasites called *Sacculina.* The *Common Prawn is* difficult to see because most of its body is almost transparent It is also able to change the spots and lines of colour marking in its body to match the background it is resting on.

Even more fascinating inhabitants of pools are the *Anemones.* The most numerous are the *Beadlet Anemones.* Their tentacles are coloured red or green and when expanded are ready to sting prey. Each sting is coiled in its cell until a hair-like trigger is touched, then a barbed thread is shot out into the victim eg. a small fish or prawn. This is then pushed into the hollow sac-like body through the mouth.

Rock pool life can vary greatly depending on the size of the pool and its position. The best to explore are probably the larger pools on the middle shore. Start with these at low tide and see how you get on. Do make sure however that you wont get cut off by the tide once it starts to come in. Happy searching!

Sea Anemones

October

October is the first full month of Autumn and gold tints are appearing on trees and in the hedgerows. This time of year is wonderfully summed up by Keats in his immortal words:

'Season of mists and mellow fruitfulness
Close bosom friend of the maturing sun'

Sadly many of our visiting summer birds will have left for warmer climes. A few House Martins however, will still be feeding late broods of chicks at the beginning of the month, but soon they will be fledged and gathering on the telephone wires before flying off to Africa.

A number of our resident birds will also start flocking at this time. In an earlier Nature Notes I mentioned a number of the splendid titles that were given to flocks of individual species of birds. I also asked readers to forward names of any other groups of birds that had not been mentioned. The following were given to me by Dick Lawrence. -

A Watch of Nightingales
A Siege of Herons
An Exaltation o f Larks
A Gaggle or Skein, or Wedge of Geese
A Piteousness of Doves
A Host of Sparrows
A Fight o f Swallows

Still mentioning birds I thought that readers would like to hear a couple of success stories about Moorhens and Canada Geese raising their young locally. Both these ground nesting birds suffer predation by local minks. However I have been informed by Pete Ray that both these species raised broods on his new pond at Hinkhams Farm this year. Because of the possibility of spreading the Foot and Mouth virus I was unable to see the young birds myself but hope that this success will be repeated next year when any threat of spreading this terrible disease has lifted.

Canada Geese and Goslings

A Pair of Moorhens

A Selection of Nature Notes Published in 2002

January

Now could be a good time to look back to see whether our local plants and animals might have been affected by *Global Warming* during the past twelve months.

Looking through my diary I recorded that I had seen *Primroses* in flower at the Five Bells Inn on the 21st January and *Snowdrops* in Shave Cross Road on the 25th. *Frogs spawn* was laid in my pond at the very beginning of February. Were these dates earlier than usual or had I been less observant in other years? Again looking at my diary I noted that the following plants were also early in flower along the Shave Cross Road:- *Colts Foot, Greater Stitchwort, Lady's Smock, Blue Bells, Wild Garlic, Garlic Mustard, Red Campion, Early Spotted Orchid* and *Cow Parsley*. If they really were earlier was this due to higher than average temperatures or was some other factor involved? Further signs of an early Spring were the appearance of *Peacock* and *Small Tortoiseshell* butterflies in early March. These probably hibernated over the Winter and would not normally have been seen on the wing before April. Their close relative the *Red Admiral* has not usually been able to survive the Winter but comes here as a migrant. There were one or two about in April however which may have survived.

Red Admirals are particularly abundant in the Autumn often seen in orchards feasting on windfalls. They were particularly numerous last Autumn and I note from my diary that a few were still about at the end of November. Did that mean that *Global Warming* might have made that Season later than usual? Certainly our local trees hung on to their leaves for much longer than in previous years and were much more brilliantly coloured. The landscape provided a veritable feast of golds. reds, ochres and siennas for several weeks. Autumn also provided a good crop of wild mushrooms. They included *Parasols, Horse Mushrooms, Shaggy Inkcaps, Giant Puffballs, Birch Boletus, Wood Blewits* and *Eared Mushrooms*. These all seemed later than usual. Most will only fruit at certain temperatures which would suggest that the soil was taking longer than normal to cool down.

This year I will keep a record of temperatures in my diary and compare them with previous averages. This should provide some concrete evidence about any real trends in local temperature changes.

A Small Tortoiseshell Butterfly

March

Many of our native amphibians will have started breeding by now. All of them lay their eggs in water. Most readers will be familiar with the mass of spawn and tadpoles of the common frog in local ponds. Some may even remember from their childhood days keeping some spawn in old jam jars, watching the tadpoles hatch and then growing legs before turning into miniature frogs.

Other amphibians produce their eggs differently. Toads lay them in a long string which is wound around plants and twigs in the water. Newts on the other hand lay their eggs singly often wrapped in the leaf of a water plant Toad spawn hatches into tadpoles which are similar to but smaller than, frog tadpoles. Toad tadpoles grow legs in the same way as frogs before they finally change into small adults. Young newts are entirely different When they hatch they already have legs and look like miniature adults with the addition of frothy gills each side of the head.

The tadpoles of both frogs and toads feed on vegetable matter until they turn into adults. Baby newts however are carnivorous from the start feeding on such things as water fleas and small worms. Frog tadpoles are often eaten by fish, the larger newts and dragonfly larvae. Toad tadpoles seem to be protected from this fate by a bitter poisonous substance which also protects them in adult life. A heron or a cat will readily eat a frog but will soon drop a toad! Newt larvae have few enemies except perhaps other newts. In this area I have only seen *common frogs, common toads* and *palmate newts*. I have been told however that *smooth newts* and the rare protected *crested newts* do appear in some of the larger ponds and lakes in the Marshwood Vale. Only frogs spawn in my garden pond together with the small *palmate newts. Toads* prefer deeper water. There are no fish in my pond and, as *palmate newts* don't seem to eat tadpoles, I am able to rear a good number of *frogs* each year.

I hope that this state of affairs will continue but I am perturbed by recent news about a virus that is killing Britain's frogs. This is said to be worse than myxomatosis, the plague that destroyed the rabbit population 40 years ago. The virus causes the frogs feet to drop off. It takes a considerable time for the animals to die and there are indications that their numbers are permanently depressed in some areas. Lets hope that it passes this area by. Fortunately it does not seem to infect toads and newts.

A Common Frog

April

As the days get warmer several of our most beautiful butterflies will wake up from their Winter hibernation, or emerge from their chrysalises, and start seeking nectar from the mass of Spring flowers that have blossomed in our gardens. Last month I wrote about the breeding habits of some of our native amphibians This month I thought that I would continue along these lines and explore the life cycle of these butterflies.

Like most insects the life of butterflies is split into four stages. In the first stage eggs are laid by the female butterfly on or near the plant that will supply food to the insect whilst it is in the caterpillar stage Once it has hatched the young caterpillar will feed on the plant until it reaches the third stage of its life when it will turn into a chrysalis Along the way it will moult a number of times, like a snake, as it outgrows its skins. When the time is right the adult butterfly will emerge from the chrysalis and, after its wings have expanded and dried, fly off in search of nectar Later it will seek a mate and indulge in a courtship flight with a possible partner, fertilization of the females eggs will take place and the whole life cycle will begin all over again.

After the adult butterfly the life stage most likely to be seen is the caterpillar They come in all sorts and sizes Some are smooth-skinned some are spiny Others are green and merge into the vegetation that they feed on. Yet others are yellow or orange or are curiously shaped The food plants chosen by these creatures also varies. Some species will only feed on one specific plant but others will survive on a number of different ones. But others will choose a plant that will provide protection against predators either by making the caterpillar inedible or providing a camouflage background for it The caterpillar of the beautiful *Orange Tip* butterfly is a good example of the use of camouflage It is on the wing in April/May and in this area lays its eggs on *Garlic Mustard* which is widespread in the verges of our local lanes The caterpillars feed on the young seedpods of this plant and lay along these pods in such a way that they look like a seedpod themselves Of all the food plants one of the most commonly used by some of our most majestic butterflies is the *Stinging Nettle*. The caterpillars of *Small Tortoiseshells, Peacocks, Commas and Red Admirals* regularly use them and sometimes *Painted Ladies*. All these caterpillars are spiney and predominately black with coloured spots or patterns They vary in their habits however. The caterpillars of the *Peacock* live in a colony until they pupate. *Small Tortoiseshells* start in a colony, which is often protected with a spun web, but they become more solitary as they grow bigger. The caterpillars of the *Red Admiral* and the *Comma* live singly.

We are lucky living where we do because *Garlic Mustard* and *Stinging Nettles* are prolific in our hedgerows and in the verges of our fields Long may they do so and provide food for the caterpillars of some of our most beautiful butterflies!

Caterpillars of the Peacock Butterfly

May

May is the month of the *Cuckoo's* song. It is one of the major signs that Spring has arrived and, over the years. it has been an inspiration for many poets and musical composers But recently a number of wildlife campaigners warned that this bird was in danger of falling silent in the British countryside because of the season—warping effect of climate change. Scientists believe global warming is causing milder Winters and early Springs. One result of this is that many trees are coming into leaf earlier and by the time the *Cuckoo* arrives the leaves are quite mature.

The favourite food of *Cuckoos* are caterpillars but if the leaves are too tough for the caterpillars to eat when they first hatch that leads to a decline in their population which has a knock-on effect for their predators.

Other signs in this country of global warming put forward by the scientists were the early appearance of a number of species of our fauna and flora. *Frog spawn* was recorded as early as last December. The *Seven-spot Ladybird* now survives the Winter by hibernating in buildings. *Bluebells* were seen in flower in March and the *Horse Chestnut* tree was in bud in late February

Locally there were also some early firsts. In my Diary I recorded seeing *Primroses* in flower in late January and *Lesser Celandine* on the 4th February. My pond was full of *frog spawn* a few days later. At the end of February *Colts Foot* was in flower in Shave Cross Road. At the beginning of March I recorded seeing a *Robin* building a nest, a new *Blackbirds* nest, a *Song Thrush's* nest with eggs and two new *Wren's* nests The Bridport News reported that a pair of *House Martins* had been seen in North Chideock. These sightings seem to confirm what the scientists are saying about the effects of global warming They are certainly earlier than when I moved to this area in 1986.

A Song Thrush's Nest

June

April saw the launch of the Garden Butterfly Count, the brainchild of Butterfly Conservation, the charity dedicated to looking after butterflies, moths and their habitats. This aims to plot a true picture of

Britain's butterfly population by recording sightings of the 22 commonest garden species and four common moths. Reports suggest that distribution patterns are changing. Butterflies such as the *Speckled Wood, Comma* and *Gatekeeper* have already started to spread further north. By asking gardeners to take part in the survey, a much clearer picture should emerge revealing which species are benefiting from climate changes and which are in decline.

The butterflies that are being covered by the survey are :- the *Brimstone, Comma, Common Blue, Green- veined White, Gatekeeper, Holly Blue, Large Skipper, Large White, Marbled White, Meadow Brown, Orange Tip, Painted Lady, Peacock, Red Admiral, Ringlet, Scotch Argus, Small Copper, Speckled Wood* and *Wall Brown*. The moths are :- the *Cinnabar, Hummingbird Hawk Moth, Magpie* and *Scarlet Tiger*. Readers wishing to take part in this survey and receive a free information pack should send their name and address (and date of birth if under 18) to:- Garden Butterflies Count, Butterfly Conservation, P0 Box 232, Melksham, Wiltshire, SN 12 7SB. Having said that it might be a good idea to start recording the butterflies in your garden now as, at the time of writing these notes, I am still waiting for my pack to arrive.

Another nature survey that took place this year was the RSPB Big Garden Birdwatch. Over 4000 people in Dorset took part in this survey an eightfold increase over the previous year's exercise. Dorset's top ten birds in order of the numbers recorded were:- the *House Sparrow, Blue Tit, Greenfinch, Blackbird, Chaffinch, Starling, Wood Pigeon, Great Tit, Robin* and *Collared Dove*. Nationally the most numerous bird was the *Starling*.

A Small Copper Butterfly

July

A couple of days after sending last month's Notes to the Editor I received my *Garden Butterflies Count* package from Butterfly Conservation. It was worth waiting for and I have no hesitation in recommending it to readers of this magazine. In addition to the survey form itself the package included a splendid *Identification Guide,* a leaflet about *Butterfly Gardening,* a *Childrens' Colouring Competition* and details of the work done by *Butterfly Conservation.* It is still not too late to take part in this survey as it continues until the end of October. The package can be obtained from The British Butterfly Conservation Ltd. Dept BGL, Manor Yard, East Lulworth, WAREHAM, Dorset, 8H20 5QP. Tel:- 01929- 400209. Go for It!

July is a very good month for looking at butterflies especially the brown butterflies, or *Satyridae* family. All of these have false eyes either on the upper or lower surface of the wings. These eyes confuse predators which gives the individual butterfly a greater chance of surviving an attack. All but one of this family is brown coloured the exception being the *Marbled White* which is white with black markings. The caterpillars of the *Browns* all eat grass. They spend the winter in the caterpillar stage and continue feeding in mild weather. There are eleven species in this family three of which occur exclusively in the north of the country. The rest can be seen in Dorset at various times of the year. In the Marshwood Vale the following *Browns* will be seen in July:- *Meadow Brown, Ringlet, Gatekeeper, Speckled Wood, Marbled White, Wall, Grayling* and *Small Heath.* Some are more common than others. There is a particularly good colony of *Graylings* on Hardown Hill where you might also see a number of *Small Heaths.*

A Speckled Wood Butterfly

September

This month I am writing about the National Marine Aquarium in Plymouth. This is the only aquarium in the UK to be run as a charity solely for education and conservation of the marine environment.

The building is laid out to show, in various sized tanks, many aspects of marine life from freshwater rivers to the deepest parts of the sea. Some of our freshwater fish such as *Perch* and *Three Spined Sticklebacks* can be seen in the first aquariums. Then there are open tanks which show marine life along the shore and in rock pools. Both of these brought back memories of childhood fishing trips and seaside holidays.

Further in there is a series of small aquariums which contain different species of Seahorses. What wonderful and strange creatures these are! With the head of a horse, the body of a caterpillar and the eyes and tail of a chameleon. They pair for life and it is the male who becomes pregnant and gives birth to as many as 1500 babies. Seahorses mainly live in warmer climes in the wild but two of the species that are kept in Plymouth can sometimes be seen in our coastal waters. Sadly between 20 or 60 million are taken from the wild each year for the Chinese medicine trade. Many others are sold as tourist trinkets. This is bringing some species to the brink of extinction. Plymouth is helping to offset this through a project aimed at breeding and rearing them in captivity. So far they have succeeded with seven species.

The other conservation project being undertaken at Plymouth is that relating to *Sharks*. The inhabitants in the Shark Theatre are all species that are known to settle well in captivity. They really are magnificent creatures to see. In the wild there are some 400 species but many are under pressure. Each year about 100 million sharks are killed world wide. It is interesting to contrast this with the 12 people who might be killed by sharks in a bad year.

The two really large exhibits at the Aquarium are the 'Deep Reef' and 'Life on the Coral Reef'. The former is based on the sea life around the Eddystone just off Plymouth and houses many large specimens such as *Pollack, Sea Bass, Corkwing* and *Ballen Wrasse.*. The later is based on a tropical coral lagoon and houses many specimens that are often only seen in televised nature programmes.

The Aquarium is well worth a visit. It can probably be seen at its best outside of the crowded holiday season.

A Seahorse

October

October is a good month for finding wild mushrooms. In an earlier Nature Notes I wrote about the edible fungi that could be found in this area and how they might be cooked. This time I am concentrating on the deadly ones.

Every year people in this country die of mushroom poisoning and many others become very ill from eating a mushroom which they thought was harmless. The most deadly are those mushrooms belonging to the *Amanita* genus. These include the *death cap*, the *panther cap*, the *destroying angel* and the *fly agaric* the red capped white spotted toadstool of fairy tales. All these fungi have white gills and a white bag-like volva around the base of the stem. Most fatal poisonings are caused by the *death cap*. It looks fairly innocuous, smells pleasant and can be peeled. Only one small cap can be fatal. It is not all that easy to identify as the cap colour can vary so much. Although there are a few good mushrooms in the Amanita group it is best to avoid this genus altogether. It is probably a good idea to avoid all white gilled mushrooms unless they are so distinctive that there is no possibility of misidentifying them e.g. the *parasol mushroom*. The *sickener* is another white gilled mushroom which is highly poisonous. It belongs to the Russula genus. This family consists of some 150 different kinds and although some are edible many are toxic. Like the *Amanita* the white gill rule should be adhered to.

Not all toxic mushrooms have white gills however and some toxic species will only affect some people or when eaten with alcohol. The *yellow -staining mushroom,* a member of the Agaric genus, looks very much like an ordinary field mushroom. The symptoms of poisoning are sweating and flushing with severe stomach cramps. Not everyone is affected but it is not worth taking any risks. Although this mushroom has many similarities to other members of the *Agaric* family one thing will readily identify it. It bruises a very bright yellow as soon as it is touched or cut. The *common ink cap* is not poisonous in itself but if eaten in conjunction with alcohol, it can cause nausea, palpitations and stomach cramps This should not be confused with the *shaggy ink cap* a readily identifiable close relative which is very enjoyable to eat with wine etc.

I have not covered all the toxic mushrooms in this article. Readers might wish to find out more about them and the good edible ones as well. The most important thing is correct. identification. A good book is an illustrated encyclopedia called Mushroom Identifier by Peter Jordan. Copies are available from the bookstall in East Street on Bridport market days for £2-99

Death Cap Mushrooms

November

In November food for many of our fauna is in short supply and this shortage will remain throughout the Winter. Most species have developed strategies for coping with this. A major one of these is *hibernation* or winter sleep.

The mammals which hibernate are mostly insect eaters such as *bats, hedgehogs* and *badgers.* Bats hibernate in sheltered dark places such as barns, attics, high up in churches and in hollow trees. Hedgehogs cover themselves with leaves and grass at the bottom of a hedgerow. Badgers take their families into their large underground dens and block up the entrances. *Squirrels* also hibernate in their dreys but not as deeply. They bury nuts in the ground for use if they wake up on warmer winter days. *Dormice* probably hibernate the deepest of all curled up in a hole or amongst the roots of a tree.

Reptiles and amphibians also employ the strategy of hibernation. *Snakes* and *lizards* rest in some dry secluded area such as under a paving stone or in a niche in a wall. *Newts* and *toads* also tend to seek out similar places. *Frogs* however will sometimes hibernate in the mud at the bottom of a pond.

Insects survive the Winter in various ways. Most butterflies and moths hibernate in the pupae stage hidden in the ground or in dense vegetation. A few such as *White Admirals* and *Purple Emperors* hibernate in the caterpillar stage and a further few in the adult stage. The later include *Peacocks, Small Tortoiseshells, Commas* and *Brimstones.* These often find shelter in our houses or outbuildings. *Red Admirals* and *Painted Ladies* may also shelter in the same places but usually will only survive in a mild Winter. *Queen Wasps* and *Bumble-bees* spend the Winter in holes in the ground. *Ladybirds* often hibernate in groups under the bark of trees or in the corner of window frames.

Birds don't hibernate. Many insect eating species survive the Winter by migrating to warmer climes. Many others rely on what food they can forage from gardens and bird tables. It is rewarding that we can help these birds by putting out food for them.Please keep up the good work.

December

The Garden Butterflies Count finished at the end of October and my survey form has been returned to Butterfly Conservation for analysis. The survey covered 22 species of common butterflies and 4 moths which might be seen in our gardens. It also asked for information about the size of the garden, the flowers it contained which would provide nectar for the adults and plants that their caterpillars could feed on. The results will be published next year.

Over the seven months survey period I was able to record sightings of 15 species of butterflies and 2 moths in my garden. These were the *Brimstone, Comma, Common Blue, Gatekeeper, Green-veined White, Holly Blue, Large White, Meadow Brown, Orange-tip, Painted Lady, Peacock, Red Admiral, Small Tortoiseshell, Small White, Speckled Wood, Humming-bird Hawk-moth* and *Magpie*. Most were seen in the Spring or Summer. By early October as temperatures fell only the Red Admiral and Speckled Wood put in an occasional appearance.

In the last week of October I spent a weeks holiday in Dubrovnic in Southern Croatia where the weather was mainly sunny and warm. There were a lot of butterflies and moths still flying about Some of these were species that could be seen earlier in the year in this country such as the *Brimstone, Clouded Yellow, Painted Lady, Red Admiral, Small White, Speckled Wood* and *Humming-bird Hawk-moth*. The moths were particularly numerous and on the occasions that we had our hotel room shutters open two or three would come in fly around as if making an inspection and then fly out again. Quite delightful! Especially as I had only seen one in Dorset this year.

There were also a number of species which are not found in this country. Some of these I was able to identify having seen them on other trips abroad. These included the *Bath White, Map Butterfly, Queen of Spain Fritillary, Two-tailed Pasha* and the *Scarce Swallowtail*. Others I could not even identify with the help of a pocket guide on European butterflies. Unfortunately I did not have my close-up camera with me so I was unable to take any photographs to aid identification when I got home.

However it was wonderful to see so many different butterflies on the wing in late October.

Green-veined White Butterfly

A Selection of Nature Notes Published in 2003

January

Many organisms are too small to be looked at without the aid of a magnifying device of some kind. Such devices include hand lenses, simple microscopes, projectors, computer microscopes, twin eye-piece and electron microscopes. Some of these can be very expensive but the simple single eye- piece microscope, or one that will project an image on to a small screen, would not break the bank and could open up a completely new world of nature. The important thing is that it should be capable of giving a range of magnifications so that it can be used to look at many different sized specimens.

Drops of river or pond water when examined with one of these devices will reveal all kinds of life. Pollen grains of different flowers and grasses can be looked at to see how they differ from one and another. Parts of insects can be seen in detail including the wings of butterflies and cross sections of plant stems and leaves can be magnified. Eggs of various moths can also be compared. The possibilities are endless.

River water will contain many Phytoplankton. Some of these microscopic algae are mobile others such as diatoms are not. Each however has its wonderful distinct shape. Pollen grains when magnified also have a rich diversity of form. Many of these are smooth but the majority have a wide range of textures. The eggs of butterflies and moths also share this diversity. Again some are smooth and round but many more are ridged or club shaped. The cross sections of plants reveal a large number of differences. Many are symmetrical but a few reveal a most haphazard pattern. Wings of butterflies are clothed in tiny scales which overlap each other like roof tiles and the whole colourful beauty of these wonderful creatures lie in these scales which contain pigments to produce colours or refract light to produce iridescent metallic hues. Each species has its own unique colouration.

Looking through a microscope and seeing all this diversity raises an age old question. Where does it all come from?

February

Some readers may be interested in taking part in one of the following wildlife surveys that are taking place this year.

Dorset Wildlife Trust is looking for volunteers to help them secure the long term survival of the *Brown Hare*. In January they launched a county wide survey to discover where these animals live in order to devise strategies for their conservation. This mammal is larger than the rabbit. It is more leggy and has much longer ears with black tips. It lives above ground rather than in burrows and sits in a hollow(form). The young are called leverets and are born furred with eyes open. The males (bucks) compete in boxing matches which has led to them being called *'Mad March Hares'*. They can best be spotted early in the morning or late evening. The Brown Hare has suffered a 75% decline in numbers since the 194Os as farming practices have changed. They are still present in Dorset but DWT are not sure where. Anyone wishing to record local sightings of this splendid animal can obtain details and recording cards from Sarah Williams, DWT Conservation Officer, on 01305- 264620.

Butterfly Conservation are running a project called *Butterflies for the New Millennium*. Records of sightings of butterflies made anywhere from gardens to mountain summits are required. The project was launched in 1995 to carry out a detailed survey of the distribution of all the butterfly species across Britain and Ireland and so provide up-to-date information for conservation and research. Anyone can help. They don't have to be experts and a free Butterflies for the Millennium information pack is available from Butterfly Conservation, Manor Yard, East Lulworth, Wareham, Dorset, BH2O 5QP.

Several people in Morcombelake have recently told me that they had spotted a Kingfisher in their garden. Is this a first for the village? I haven't seen one since coming to Dorset and I would be interested to hear about any other sightings of this wonderful bird.

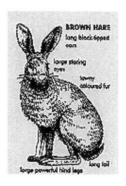

Dorset Wildlife Trust's Hare Recognition Chart

April_____

There was a report in the press recently about a catastrophic fall in the number of woodland birds. Some ornithologists have blamed this on wild deer and have called for a nationwide deer cull by trained sharpshooters. Many senior naturalists believe that the culling of many thousands of deer will be needed to prevent many of Britain's woodland birds such as *Song Thrushes, Lesser Spotted Woodpeckers,*

Bullfinchs, Willow Tits and *Marsh Tits* from going into decline.

Evidently there has been a huge increase in the numbers of *Munjac, Roe* and *Fallow Deer* over the past few decades due to modem farming practices and warmer weather. This increase in numbers is being blamed for damaging the broadleaf woods and forests that numerous birds rely on by grazing on saplings, lower leaves and underbrush.

Some bird species have declined in numbers by almost 60% since the early 1970s. *Willow Tit* numbers have fallen by 78%, *Lesser Spotted Woodpeckers* by 62% and *Song Thrushes* by over one half. Last year nine threatened woodland birds were added to the 'red list' of endangered species, leading the Forestry Minister to spend £600,000 on attempts to discover the scale and cause of the problem The study starts this Spring when experts from the RSPB and the British Trust for Ornithology will begin surveying bird numbers in 350 woods across Britain. Although deer pressure is their favorite hypothesis they will explore several other theories on the cause of the decline, including, changes in farming practice, egg stealing by *Grey Squirrels* etc. competition for available seeds and global warming. Nobody wants to see Deer being completely eliminated if a cull goes ahead. The question is what would be the optimum number that will be in balance with the biodiversity of our woods.

The question of culling is always raised when the numbers of one species increase to the detriment of other species in the same environment. It often raises great emotion such as the proposed culling of *Hedgehogs* on an island in Scotland because they were so numerous that they were decimating the number of sea bird by eating most of their eggs. Perhaps some readers will agree that such culling is necessary.

Roe Deer in a Local Garden

Photograph by Cunningham Hill

June

In previous Nature Notes I have written about the creatures found in garden ponds that depend on water for certain stages of their lives. These include frogs, toads, newts, dragonflies, damselflies and caddis-flies. This month I am exploring the lives of some of our fauna who spend all or most of their lives in our ponds.

Some water-bugs such as *Pond Skaters* live on the surface-film of the water. They can be seen gracefully skating about on the surface of ponds in search of food. They are carnivorous insects who suck out the blood of other animals. Their young resemble the adults. There is no pupal stage. Another member of this family is the *Water Boatman* who as a rule swims just under the surface of the water upside down. This creature is a strong swimmer. It takes on quite large prey and can inflict a very painful bite.

Living in the main body of water below the surface are a number of water beetles the largest of which is the *Great Diving Beetle*. They are ruthless predators. The large suckers on the front legs of the male beetles are used for gripping the females when mating. Their eggs are laid in the stems of water plants. The larvae are also ruthless predators with powerful jaws. Both the adult and the larva need to rise for air. Another beetle is the *Whirligig* which spends most of its time gyrating on the surface but dives when disturbed. Its eyes are divided so the upper half see above the water and the lower half below it. Both the *Water Boatman* and the *Beetles* are able to fly so this is how they spread from pond to pond.

A further group of animals to be seen in ponds are the water snails. The *Great Pond Snail* is the largest of the pulmate snails its shell spiraling to a point.It feeds on plants but also scavenges on newts and small fish. Another pulmonate is the *Ramshorn Snail* This has a spiral shell resembling a sheep's horn. This snail is not as common as other snails and is much prized by aquarists. It only feeds on plants. Both of these snails have to rise to the surface of the water for air.

The debris that collects in the bottom of ponds provides a habitat for many other creatures. These include a number of *Freshwater Shrimps* who scavenge in it and small *Freshwater Mussels* who spend their life buried in it. This debris also provides shelter and food for several kinds of worms.

A Water Boatman

August

This month I am writing about some of our larger moths and their caterpillars especially the splendid Hawk-moth family. With the exception of a few species most of these are on the wing during the hours of darkness and it is their caterpillars which will be spotted more often than the adults. Some are very rare e.g. the *Death's-head Hawkmoth* and are unlikely to occur in this area. Night flying species which might put in an appearance however include, *Lime Hawkmoths, Poplar Hawkmoths, Eyed Hawkmoths* , both of the *Elephant Hawkmoths* and rarely the largest member of the family the *Convolvulus Hawkmoth*. The caterpillars of the first three look very similar. They are green bodied with white side stripes and have the characteristic Hawkrnoth's horn at the end of their bodies.. If such caterpillars are found feeding on the leaves of a lime tree they will be the larvae of *Lime Hawkmoths* as these leaves are their only food The caterpillars of the other two will feed on the leaves of the same trees such as Poplar, Willow, Aspen and Sallow so identification can be difficult. The *Elephant Hawkmoth* and the *Small Elephant Hawkmoth* also have similar caterpillars both being elephant grey in colour with a small horn at the rear and eye-spots near the head. The former feeds on Willowherbs however and the later on Bedstraws. The day flying species that might be seen on the wing are the *Humming-bird Hawkmoth, the Broad-bordered Bee Hawkmoth* and the *Narrow-bordered Bee Hawkmoth.*

One of the most spectacular caterpillars of the larger moths is that of the *Puss Moth* a member of the prominent family. This caterpillar has a unique way of fending off predators. When threatened it puffs up and shoots out red filaments from twin horns at the end of its tail and spurts out jets of formic acid from its mouth. Not many predators are able to deal with this and most caterpillars survive. When they pupate they spin a cocoon rather like that of a silkworm which again gives protection during the winter months.

Another interesting moth is the *Garden Tiger*. These are remarkable for their nocturnal flight pattern. They are not attracted to light until about midnightl but then they come swarming in great numbers. The caterpillar is the 'woolly bear' of our childhood. A recent newspaper article reported that some scientists were worried that there has been a decline in the numbers of many of our Larger moths e.g the population of the *Garden Tiger Moth* has declined by 44% and some other moths by much more. They thought that climate change and the wetter warmer winters Britain was experiencing might be implicated.The *Garden Tiger* overwlnters as a caterpillar and it may be subject to fungal attack in the damp conditions.

A Convolvulus Hawk-moth

September

Owls are fascinating creatures. They are different from most other birds in that they hunt in darkness and sleep during the day Their eyes are at the front of their head rather than at the side which gives them binocular vision which enables them to judge distances with precision The disadvantage of using forward looking eyes is overcome by the ability to turn their head through 180 degrees which enables them to see directly behind them. They have excellent hearing and their soft feathers give noiseless flight. Owls feed mainly on the larger insects and small mammals such as mice, voles and shrews. The prey is usually swallowed whole. Indigestible parts such as fur, bones and beetle wing cases are regurgitated in the form of pellets.

The following species occur in southern England:- *Tawny Owl, Barn Owl, Little Owl, Long- eared Owl* and *Short -eared Owl.* Of these I have spotted the first three in the Marshwood Vale. The Long-eared Owl tends to inhabit conifer woods and might occur in this area. Short-eared Owls however are birds of open country living on dunes, marshes moors etc..and probably might not be seen here. The Tawny Owl, which is sometimes called the Brown Owl, is the most numerous owl in this country numbering about 20,000 breeding pairs. It is heard most often in the autumn when territories are being established. The call of this owl has been described as 'to-whit-to-woo' but this sound is made by two birds. One bird hoots and the shrill kwick-kwick' is the answering call of the mate. This species usually nest in hollow trees where two to four white eggs are laid in March and the young fly in about eight or nine weeks. The number of Barn Owls declined in many parts of the country during the second half of the last century because of the modernization of barns where they nested and the covering of belfries with wire netting. Things have improved however since then because many farmers are putting owl nesting boxes in their barns. Present numbers are estimated to be about 4,000 breeding pairs and rising. The number of Little Owls at present is thought to be in the region of 6,000 breeding pairs.

Owls are portrayed in ancient myths and over the centuries they have inspired many poets, writers, artists, craftsmen and toy makers in their work. This relationship between nature and art is a theme I would like to return to in a future Nature Notes.

November

In previous Nature Notes I have written about fungi and when and where they might be seen in this area. Details of both edible and poisonous varieties were given. All those I described had English names such as *Wood Blewit, Fly Agaric, Giant Puffball, Shaggy Inkcap* and *Chicken of the Woods*. However in fact only about a hundred of the thousand commoner species found in this country have such English titles and the rest have long scientific names in Latin. All this is to change however. In an attempt to make fungi more accessible to non-specialists, and foster more interest in them English Nature, Scottish Natural Heritage and the wildflower charity Plantlife International, have joined forces with the British Mycological Society to produce a list of acceptable English names for the rest of these commoner species. The names were drawn up by Elizabeth Holden, a Scottish based mycologist, using a combination of old and new guides to fungi and also her imagination. So fungi known by the Latin name of *Bisporella citrina* are now called **Lemon Disco**, *Bjerkandera adjusta* are now **Smokey Brackets**, *Cudonia confusa* is **Cinnamon Jellybaby**, *Verpa conica* are **Thimble Morel**, *Hyphodontia sambuci* are **Elder Whitewash** and *Phellodon niger* are **Black Tooth**. These names seem very apt and I look forward to them being used in any new guides about our native species.

Fungi, which can also be called mushrooms or toadstalls, are unique in that they cannot really be referred to as flora. None of them contain the green pigment chlorophyll so they cannot make their own food by the process known as photosynthesis. None are green in the sense that a tree or flowering plant is. They get their nourishment from dead organisms, excrement, dead vegetation etc or by being parasites on living plants and trees. Mushrooms are normally defined as the edible, spore-producing bodies of some edible fungi. The term toadstool on the other hand is applied to the spore -producing bodies of fungi that are not only inedible but may also be highly dangerous.

One way to observe how quickly these fruiting bodies appear is to grow field mushrooms at home. Kits for growing them are available from Garden Centres and Seed Merchants. It is quite magical to see how quickly the fruiting bodies swell from pinhead size to large flat headed specimens. Last year I obtained from Dobies Seeds wooden plugs which contained the spores of *Oyster Mushrooms* and *Shitaki Mushrooms*. These were placed in holes drilled in freshly cut logs. The logs were first placed in black sacks for four months and then planted out in the garden according to Dobies' instructions. These logs should now produce mushrooms several times a year for up to five years. At the time of writing I have had a large number of Oyster Mushrooms growing. Shitaki mushrooms however take longer and, fingers crossed, should start producing next Spring.

Oyster Mushrooms

January

Many of our small mammals are not seen as often as our birds and butterflies. This is particularly true of voles and shrews which are mainly seen as mangled corpses that have been brought indoors by family cats

Voles are small rodents with blunt snouts, small ears end short tails. There are four kinds of votes in the UK. One is confined to the Orkney Isles and Guernsey. Of the others the *Field Vole,* sometimes called the Short-tailed Vole, is the commonest mammal in the country. In a normal year they number some 75 million. They are widespread in rough pasture, plantations, heaths and woodland glades where they feed mainly on grass and roots. The colour of their coat is a dark mixture of black and brown with a touch of grey on the flanks. The colour of their slightly larger relative the *Bank Vole,* is more rusty red and brown in colour. This relative is a lowland vole which inhabits mixed woodlands, hedgerows and ground vegetation. It feeds mainly on seeds, buds and berries which can sometimes make it a pest in gardens. The population of this vole number some 23 million at the beginning of the breeding season. Voles are closely related to lemmings and like them experience regular booms and busts in their populations The large numbers of these voles provide regular food for predators from foxes to owls, weasels and adders. Many opportunist predators such as magpies, crows and badgers also eat them. The *Water Vole,* Ratty in 'Wind in the Willows', is perhaps the most well known member of this family largely because of the big decline in its numbers caused by escaped mink. Being about the same size as a rat it has also been persecuted in the past because of mistaken identity. This is a pity because it is a harmless creature that cause no problems for us. This vole is usually found close to water along the edge of slow running streams, canals, lakes and marshes. It feeds on waterside plants, bark and water snails. Recently it has been suggested that the decline in numbers might be turned around. This is because it is thought that the numbers of mink might decline as otters, who are their natural enemies, make their own comeback. Also the Wildlife Trusts have started a campaign to prevent confusion between water voles and rats which has been taken up by the main pest control agencies.

Shrews are mainly insect eaters and can be seen as being beneficial to farmers and gardeners. There are three kinds of shrew in Britain. The *Common Shrew* has a somewhat mouse-like build with a heavily whiskered pointed snout and small ears. Its fur is short and coloured rusty brown turning to white underneath. It is widespread in hedgerows, woods and plantations. This shrew is hunted and eaten by owls but is otherwise left alone when killed because of its musty smell. The *Pygmy Shrew* is the smallest British mammal. It is similar to the common shrew in its habits and just as widespread. The colour of its fur is paler and its tail longer. The *Water Shrew* is the largest of the British shrews. This animal is very much confined to the waterside, usually of slow-running streams. Stiff hairs grow under its tail and hind legs which aid swimming. Its fur is a dark slate colour with white below. I have never spotted one of these creatures so I am not sure whether or not it is native to this area

A Young Short-tailed Vole

February

The effects of climate change on our wildlife seem to be more noticeable every year. Winters are moving into Spring earlier and nature's clock seems to have gone awry as birds, bees and flowers respond to the warmer days. A survey carried out by members of the Woodland Trust last year found that on average insects were three weeks early and plants were two weeks ahead in terms of leafing and flowering. Spring migrant birds arrived at least a week earlier and stayed for longer.

Meteorological Office records showed that compared with the average temperatures for the years 1961-1990, January was 2 degrees Celsius higher, February 3.2 degrees, March 2.5 degrees and April 1.4 degrees. May however was only 0.7 degrees higher and June a mere 0.1 degrees. It seems that the weather in the earlier months was a deciding factor in how soon natural events began in the Spring. It was thought that once the process was set in motion it seemed to continue. For example, *Dog Roses* and *Ox-eye Daisies* were both in bloom about two weeks early despite the fact that temperatures in their flowering period - May and June -were closer to average. It was the same with insects. Butterflies such as *Small Tortoiseshells, Commas*, and *Peacocks* were seen much earlier than usual. *Bumble Bees* were busy some fifteen days ahead of schedule and common birds e.g. *Blackbirds* and *Blue Tits* nested eight or nine days earlier than usual

Climate change may also be the reason that some of our Spring migrant birds have been staying on as residents here. These are said to include warblers such as the *Blackcap* and *Chiff-chaff*. Other species may be recorded as the result of the RSPB's Big Garden Bird Watch which takes place this month. Some of our migrant butterflies may be surviving the warmer winters here and raising earlier broods e.g. *Red Admirals* and *Painted Ladies*

The warmer temperatures combined with transatlantic winds have resulted in sightings of a number of exotic North American birds being spotted in the UK. In the South West these included an *American Robin*, an *American Widgeon* , a *Green-winged teal* and a *Lesser Yellowlegs* at Hayle in Cornwall. In Dorset a *Lesser Scaup* was seen at Studland. There were also sightings of some rare warblers which normally live in South East Asia i.e. a *Dusky Warbler* near Paignton and a *Yellow-browed Warbler* at Lychett Bay. Exotic fish were also found in growing numbers off the coast of Cornwall which biologists at the Plymouth Marine Laboratory have linked to rising temperatures in the North Atlantic Ocean.

A Dog Rose

April

Before writing this month's article I did some research on beetles and particularly common beetles that might be seen in this country.

Beetles are the largest group of insects in the world. There are over 250,000 species, of which an estimated 3,700 can be found in the British Isles. Like most insects, beetles have two pairs of wings but only the hind ones are used for flying. The front wings are hardened into wing cases that protect the body and delicate hind wings when the insect is not flying. These wing cases are often brightly coloured. The beetle's life cycle includes an egg, larva, pupa and adult stage They are usually divided into the following groups:

a) **Carnivores**   b)**Wood-eaters** c) **Plant feeders**
d) **Scavengers**   e) **Water beetles**

I have written about water beetles in an earlier article, so these Notes will only cover the first four groups

The **Carnivores** include the *Devil's Coach Horse, Tiger Beetle, Ladybird, Glow-worm* and *Snail Beetle*. The larva and adults feed on other insects and in many cases are beneficial to man. This is especially true in the case of Ladybirds who consume vast quantities of aphids.

. The **Wood-eaters** are not so beneficial and in many cases are serious pests. These include the *Elm Bark Beetle, Deathwatch Beetle, Furniture beetle, Long Horn Beetle* and *Stag Beetle*. Some readers will be familiar with the ravages of the larva of some of these insects!

. Some of the **Plant Feeders** are also pests. These include the *Cockchafer, Rose Beetle, Oil Beetle, Blister Beetle, Click Beetle* and *Vine Weevil*. The larva of the latter is a particular nuisance as some gardeners will know!

The **Scavengers** include the *Ground Beetle, Burying Beetle, Churchyard Beetle, Dung Beetle,* and the aptly named *Scavenger Beetle,*. By and large these are useful insects who do a good job in getting rid of a lot of waste matter.

A Male Stag Beetle

May

The results of the RSPB's Big Garden Birdwatch 2004 have now been published. Altogether over 409,000 people participated in the exercise and they observed over 6 million birds. A number of species of birds were found to have declined in numbers. Others were found to have increased their populations. The losers included the *Starling, House Sparrow. Song Thrush* and *Blackbird*. Some of the winners are the *Woodpigeon, Collard Dove, Greenfinch* and *Great Tit*.

The survey found that the *House Sparrow* is the most numerous bird in the country as a whole overtaking the *Starling* that was the most common bird last year. This is not because the number of *House Sparrows* had increased but because their numbers have declined at a lower rate than the *Starling*. i.e.52% against 71% since the first Big Garden Birdwatch in 1979.These two species join two other familiar birds, the *Blackbird* and *Song Thrush* as the biggest losers since 1979,the former by 31% and the latter by 34%. By contrast two members of the pigeon family, once much less familiar in gardens, have led the success stories by showing remarkable increases. The *Woodpigeon* has increased by525% since 1979 and the *Collared Dove* by a similar amount. The *Green Finch* has increased by 84% in the last 25 years and the *Great Tit* by 65%. These increases are thought to be partly due to the increasing amounts of food that people are putting out in their gardens for birds. The findings of a recent survey into the numbers of sea birds in the UK that were presented to the 8th International Seabird Conference in Aberdeen showed that the number of seabirds around our coasts have increased from 5 million to an astonishing 8 million over the past 30 years. Again there have been winners and losers. The winners include the *Common Guillemot* whose numbers have risen to 1.6 million, the *Fulmer* and the *Puffin* whose numbers have topped the million mark. On the losing side there are three species of terns, The *Little Tern, Artic Tern* and *Sandwich Tern. Kittiwakes* and *Shags* have also declined in numbers. It is thought that some of this decline might be due to a decrease in the number of sand eels available, which form a major part of the diet of these birds.

A Great Tit

June

Last month I gave the results of two surveys about the populations of British birds in gardens and around the coasts. This month's Notes is about surveys of butterflies, moths and other flying insects.

The Garden Butterflies Count 2003, which was organized by the charity Butterfly Conservation, showed that the top 14 most common garden butterflies and moths in the country were as follows:—

1. Red Admiral
2. Large White
3.Small White
4. Small Tortoiseshell
5. Peacock
6. Painted Lady
7. Comma
8. Meadow Brown

9. Gatekeeper
10. Orange-tip
11. Speckled Wood
12. Brimstone
13. Holly Blue
14. Humming-bird Hawk-moth

Almost all of the 26 species included in the survey were seen in more gardens than in a similar survey in 2002, with only the Holly Blue and the Magpie moth declining slightly. The biggest increases were in the number of Painted Ladies and Humming-bird Hawk-moths seen. According to the sightings recorded another group of butterflies that did particularly well in 2003 were the rarer garden species. The Small Copper probably did best amongst this group, increasing from being seen in 19% of gardens in 2002 to 30% in 2003. Others that did well included the Small Skipper and Common Blue. All these increased by more than a third. Good news indeed!

Another insect survey called the Big Bug Count is being arranged in June by the RSPB. Birds such as Swallows, House Martins and Spotted Flycatchers depend on insects. Many of the birds and the insects they eat are declining. The reasons are not known and the RSPB hope that the Big Bug Count will help them to understand about insect numbers. Basically, interested parties in this survey are asked to use a provided splatometer' which helps to count the number of insects caught on your car's numberplate. Details from The RSPB, Freepost NAT 15594, Bedford. MK42 OBR if you wish to take part.

A Common Blue Butterfly

July

Before starting some of my Nature Notes I have to carry out a lot of research into the subject I plan to write about, This is a learning process for me as well as many of my readers. For this month's article I have researched into the life of spiders.

Evidently there are over 20,000 species of spiders in the world. Over 600 of these have been recorded in the British Isles. All these spiders have a poison bite with which they subdue their prey. But in spite of the fear many people have of them, no British spiders are harmful to man. These creatures which are *Arachnids* should not be confused with insects. Instead of antennae they have sensory palps. They also have a pair of fangs and four pairs of walking legs. All are carnivorous taking in pre-digested liquid food. Spiders spin silk from spinnerets at the end of their bodies which is used for various webs and traps for catching prey. These creatures perform an elaborate courtship of visual displays such as touching and vibrating their webs. After mating the male usually dies from exhaustion. Some of the more common species to be seen in this area are described below.

The *House Spider* is a long legged, fast moving hunter usually found in buildings , sometimes scaring occupants when it appears in the bath or basin. It lives in a funnel at the base of a triangular-shaped web in some odd corner. The web is covered with trip-wires over the entrance, the so called cobweb. The *Garden Spider,* sometimes called the orb spider, builds an elaborate circular web seen in gardens and hedgerows, especially in late summer when these are covered in dew. It is a masterpiece of design, made by instinct in an hour or less. The spider then hides, holding a connecting thread to maintain contact with the web. The *Money Spider* is popularly associated with wealth and responsible for the clouds of gossamer seen drifting in the air. A hammock-shaped web is constructed in the autumn in long grass, low undergrowth etc. and is more readily visible during frost or after heavy dew. This spider may travel long distances carried aloft on silk by the

A Garden Spider

August

This month I am writing about the **LIVING CHURCHYARDS PROJECT,** why it was set up and what problems it hopes to overcome.

I. **THE PROBLEMS.** In the last thirty years or so, 95% of England's herb-rich meadowland, with its support for insects, birds and small mammals, has been lost. In the same period, much farmland, both arable and grazed, has lost its ability to support wildlife and a very high percentage of hedgerows has been grubbed out.

2. WHY CHURCHYARDS? Churchyards are an important refuge for wild-life, containing a wide diversity of meadow and woodland plants. The seed banks in many churchyards are over 1000 years old, forming a rich potential if conditions are right. Insects, small mammals and birds find a home in these places, where an absence of ploughing and chemicals has formed a welcome oasis for wildlife in an increasingly hostile environment.

3. WHY SHOULD WE BE INVOLVED?
a.God has given us stewardship of his earth; it is our Christian duty to respect and protect it.
b. The future quality of human life is dependent on the preservation of biodiversity.
c. A 'Living Churchyard' can be a dignified and warm environment, which speaks of new life, hope and peace

Last year marked the 10th anniversary of the Living Churchyards Project in Dorset This Project is a national initiative, initially supported by the National Agricultural Centre and by the churches of the country. It is usually operated by the County Wildlife Trusts and, in Dorset as in other dioceses, is supported by the Diocesan Bishop, the Bishop of Salisbury. The objective of the Project is to raise awareness of the growing importance of churchyards and other burial grounds as havens of wildlife in an increasingly hostile environment, and to advise on and encourage their maintenance with wildlife in mind, without losing sight of their primary function as dignified resting places for the dead and places of peace and comfort for those who mourn.

Ways to achieve this in Dorset include the following:

1)An annual competition of churchyards, with classes for 'Best Managed for Wildlife', 'Best New Entry' and 'Best Urban'. Each entrant receives an attractive report, with details of resources discovered and advice for future management, together with a printed card for the porch, to inform visitors of the church's support for the project.

2) A system of Seminars , throughout the county, at which church representatives can ask questions and exchange experiences.

3) Advice on request, on setting up a management plan and drawing up a list of what the churchyard contains in terms of plants and other wild life. An annual newsletter, containing lists of activities and resources and a range of leaflets on specific aspects of the task.

4) Ongoing support and advice, on demand, on local difficulties and needs. It is hoped to expand this area of work and to provide training days from time to time, for those who wish to go more deeply into the scheme.

The Dorset Wildlife Trust can give advice on a wide range of relevant subjects; and can be contacted on 01305- 264620. Michael and Janet Homewood can be reached for matters relating to the project on 01929 556216.

September

At the moment my garden pond is full of overgrown water plants such as *Water Milfoil* and *Canadian Pond Weed*. Last year this was kept under control by large numbers of frog and toad tadpoles feeding on it, but this year there were none to be seen. Some frogs-spawn was laid in the pond during the last week in January and I was also given some from neighbouring ponds by friends who didn't want their fish to eat it. Altogether I must have put ten or more clumps of spawn in my pond but no tadpoles hatched from it. Later I tried to obtain some tadpoles from local lakes where in previous years I had seen myriads of both frog and toad tadpoles. There were very few to be seen this year. One possibility may have been that there was a very cold snap shortly after the frogs spawn was laid which may have stopped it hatching. Toads spawn however is normally laid later than frogs spawn so it wouldn't have been affected by the cold snap. I spoke to a number of people about the lack of tadpoles to be seen and most of them said they had noticed this but could offer no possible explanation for it. A letter in a gardening magazine however mentioned that the writer had seen *Great Pond Snails* in her pond feeding on the clumps of spawn that had been laid there and that no tadpoles hatched from it. My pond is home to a large number of snails and it is possible that they may have eaten the spawn before it could hatch. I am loath to cull these snails so next year I plan to hatch any spawn in buckets of rainwater and then transfer the mobile tadpoles to the pond. The buckets can be protected from any heavy frost by using fleece to cover them. I shall give the results of this experiment in a later Nature Notes next year.

A short while ago my neighbour showed me a young *Grass Snake* that he disturbed in his garden. This was the first time I had seen this snake since coming to Dorset The only reptiles I had seen in this area before had been *Slow-Worms* which are quite common. The young *Grass Snake* was about the same size and colour but could easily be identified by the two yellow thumb prints behind its head. A few weeks later I saw a much larger specimen in the field opposite. Both *Slow-Worms* and *Grass Snakes* are harmless creatures who do a lot of good in the garden. I look forward to spying more of them.

. There seen to have been a large number of *Swallows* about this year. Early in August a large flock appeared on our thatched roof and started prising insects out of the reed. They then started to perch in lines on the overhead electric cables opposite as if they were preparing to fly back to their Winter homes in North Africa. Whether this was the case I don't know. I know that the adult birds usually leave earlier than their offspring but this seems very early to me.

The dull weather in July seemed to affect the numbers of mid-summer butterflies that could be seen on the wing. Only the *Meadow*

Browns and *Gatekeepers* appeared to be near their normal numbers. I spotted no *Ringlets* or *Graylings* and only a few *Marbled Whites* could be seen in their normal habitats in the area. The buddleia and bramble flowers, which normally attract many butterflies to their nectar in July, only had a few specimens feeding off of them. This apparent lack of butterflies was noticed by other people in the village who mentioned it to me. I don't know however whether or not this was a general pattern elsewhere in Dorset.

A Marbled White Butterfly

October

Further to previous information about Dorset Wildlife Trust's Living Churchyard Project I am delighted to have learnt that our wonderful churchyard of St. Candida and Holy Cross has been accepted as the Best Newcomer to the Project. I hope more details will be available later.

One of the things mentioned by the Trust was that there was a good display of lichen in the churchyard. This observation has led me to do some research into lichen and other lower plants a subject that hitherto has been a mystery to me. What a fascinating area of plant life it turned out to be! I discovered that the lower plants include *Lichens, Mosses, Liverworts, Clubmosses* and *Algae*.

Lichens are actually a combination of two plants, fungus and algae. The former produces fruit and the latter food. They are usually paler than mosses, greyer, but some with bright splashes of fruit bodies. Lichens take many forms some flat and encrusted on rocks, barks and gravestones, others more bushy and attached to branches. They are rootless, water being absorbed through their surfaces. They are very sensitive to pollution and mainly occur in the cleaner, wetter west and north.

Mosses are a primitive group of small green, flowerless plants, with pointed leaves encircling the stem. Wind-blown spores germinate into new plants. They grow close together in dense colonies almost anywhere - on the ground, walls, trees, rocks, even in water(e.g. willow moss) and bogs (sphagnum moss). There is an alternation of generations i.e. there is an asexual spore-producing stage, followed by a sexual stage. There are about 600 species in the UK.

Clubmosses are creeping, spore-bearing perennials somewhat moss-like but more robust, with small pointed leaves which overlap and encircle the stem. Spore cases are at the base of the leaves in erect cones. They mainly grow in rough pasture on mountain slopes, moors and heaths. There are six British species.

Liverworts are small spore-bearing, flowerless plants that can be mistaken for mosses, mostly without upright stems or leaves. A few leafy species have rounded leaves and most consist of flat fronds with slender rootlets resembling lobes of liver. They have alternating generations like mosses. Generally found in damp places e.g. ditches, drains, bogs, by streams and on rotting wood. There are over 200 species in Britain.

Algae are the simplest of plants that are mainly aquatic, ranging from one-celled forms to large seaweeds. All contain chlorophyll which may be masked with red or brown pigments. There are numerous microscopic forms which swim actively with whip-like threads. Others form filamented threads of cells end to end and become blanket weed which sometimes chokes a pond.

Lichen on Tree Bark

A Selection of Nature Notes Published in 2005

February

Recently an article was published in the Bridport News about the number of birds that had been seen migrating from Dorset via West Bay last year. The number of species spotted and the number of individual birds counted were quite staggering so I thought that I should write about the phenomenon in this month's 'Nature Notes'. West Bay, as in previous years, provided the run-way for a huge migration of land birds last Autumn with experts recording some of the biggest movements of birds in the UK. Close to a 100.000 were observed passing through by Bridport based ecologist Dr Tom Brereton and West Bay birdwatcher Tony Warren. Thousands more are thought to have migrated from the resort unspotted. The following reasons were put forward as to why they were missed:-

a)Most of the activity occurs in the first couple of hours after dawn, the birds are often relatively high up and they can be further inconspicuous as many of the flocks are small;

b) It is also the case that many of the migrants were familiar birds such as *Greenfinches, Chaffinches* and *Goldfinches.* which are often not thought of as seasonal migrants. and the little flocks seen might have been dismissed as the same local birds;

c) many birds such as *Thrushes, Robins* and *Warblers* migrate at night, passing silently in the dark skies.

Those migrating through the day (the diurnal migrants) however were easily spotted. The top of the west cliff at West Bay, the Devil's Dip, offered a panoramic view point in all directions and this, combined with its proximity to the coast, made it the ideal platform to watch these birds leaving. By far and away the main form of migration witnessed was 'coasting,' where the birds head into the wind gaining lift. and then following the coastline to use it as a navigational aid. On far fewer occasions birds were also seen heading out to sea or coming in from the sea. The conditions favoured for migration by most species were when there were light to moderate winds and the sky was clear and sunny. On such days it was not unusual to see thousands of birds coasting west one day into the west wind, then the following day to see an equal number of birds coasting east into an east wind.

The migration began in August when flocks of *Wagtails, Hirundines* and *Pipits* were observed moving south en-route from their breeding grounds in Scandinavia. Iceland and Britain to their wintering grounds in southern Europe and Africa. Large numbers of *Swallows* and *House Martins* built up over the south coast in early September. Movements of these species lasted all day with perhaps 10.000 or more birds moving during peak days. Mid to late September saw the peak migration of *Meadow Pipits* flying wave after wave of small groups, totalling 2000 birds every hour or so. October was without doubt the peak month for migration both In terms of the number and variety of birds. The big movers included *Pied Wagtails, Starlings, Skylarks* and various *Thrushes, Finches* and *Buntings*. The first half of the month had frequent windy weather- conditions largely unsuitable for migration. Light westerly winds and sunny spells however, from the 16th to the 18th provided a long awaited window of opportunity for eager migrant birds that had been held up by the earlier strong winds. Over the three days 15,000 birds moved through. most of them, coasting west. These included 3.800 *Greenfinches*, 2.200 *Chaffinches*, 1.700 *Meadow Pipits*, 1.000 *Linnets*. 1.200 *Wagtails* and 3,000 *Skylarks*. With a further spell of windy weather things went on hold. The week following the 26th however saw more than 50,000 birds passing through including 36.000 *Starlings* and the first substantial autumn movement of *Jackdaws, Pigeons*. and *Scandinavian Thrushes*. Then things quietened down in November. The yearly figures included exceptional counts by West Dorset standards for *Starlings* (45,OOO), *Greenfinches* (9.800), *Skylarks* (4,800), *Chaffinches* (5.200) and *Reed Warblers* (350).

The sightings made raise a lot of interesting unanswered questions as to the origins and ultimate destination of the birds i.e. they demonstrate that there is still much to learn about the migrations of some of our most familiar species and that exciting discoveries can be made on our doorstep.

A Cock Chaffinch

March

In March, Spring really gets underway. Birds are nesting and many wild flowers are in bloom. Recently I was given a book of poems by John Clare who was a great chronicler of nature at this time of the year. Many of his poems are about birds, their nests and eggs, and others are about wild flowers. Some are based on childhood memories and some on later experiences. Birds described in his poems include the *Crow, Sand Martin, Skylark, Snipe, Wren* and *Yellowhammer*. The following part of one about the Wren really struck a chord.

Why is the Cuckoo's melody preferred
And Nightingale's rich song so often praised
In poets rhymes? Is there no other bird
Of natures minstrelsy that oft hath raised
One's heart to ecstasy and mirth as well?
I judge not how another's taste is caught
With mine there's other birds that bear the bell
Whose song hath crowds of happy memories brought
Such the wood robin singing in the dell
And little wren that many a time hath sought
Shelter from showers in huts where I did dwell

When writing poems about nests he sometimes refers to the
parent birds by a local name. Thus *a Willow Warbler* is referred to
as **a** Pettichap and a *Long Tailed Tit* a Bumbarrel. Other poems
refer to the nests of *Blackbirds, Linnets, Moorhens, Song Thrushes* and
Yellowhammers. The following verses from a poem about
childhood memories encompasses several of these

And o'er the firsts bumbarrel's nest
We wondered at the spell
That birds who served no prenticeship
Could build their nests so well
And finding linnet's moss was green
And finches choosing grey
And every finch's nest alike
Our wits were blown away

Then blackbirds lining theirs with grass
And thrushes theirs with dung
So for our lives we could not tell
From whench the wisdom sprung
We marveled much how little birds
Should ever be so wise
And so we guessed some angel came
To teach them from the skies

A Blackbird's Nest

April

Bats are the only mammals capable of true flight Their wings consist of membranes stretched between much elongated fingers and connecting along the sides of the body the hind legs and most of the tail. Their hook-like thumbs and hind toes are used for crawling and gripping on to resting places. All bats in this country hunt insects and hibernate in winter.

All 16 species of bats have been recorded in Dorset usually roosting in buildings and trees, but also in caves tunnels and other underground structures. The most commonly recorded species is the *Pipistrelle*. which is scattered throughout all of the county; the *Long-eared* Bat throughout rural Dorset: and the *Serotine* which is concentrated around north and west Dorset. The less common species include *Barbastelle, Bechstein's, Brandt's, Daubenton's, Greater Horseshoe, Lesser Horseshoe, Natterer's, Noctule* and *Whiskered Bats.* Bats are animals of major ecological importance as the major predators of night- flying insects. Centuries of myth and legend have given them a greatly undeserved bad reputation as in reality they are amongst the most beneficial creatures on earth. All of our species of bats are of international importance. and are protected by domestic. European and international law.

Bats require different roosting conditions at different times of the year and will therefore move regularly to find the right conditions. In the UK. bat roosts have been reported in a great variety of places, but generally they can be split into three groups, buildings, trees and underground structures. Some bats will roost in our houses and so their conservation depends very much on our tolerance and good will. They also roost in other buildings, new and old including churches. Those roosting in trees can sometimes be disturbed by damaging operations such as tidying up branches. Underground roosts can be in tunnels, caves, ruins and cellars etc. and these can sometimes be disturbed by maintenance routines or by entrances being blocked off.

More detailed information about bats is given in a number of English Nature leaflets that can be obtained from Dorset Wildlife Trust. These include guidelines which aim to provide planning officers and councillors with the information needed to consider the effects of planning and development on bats. They cover identification of sites used by bats, appropriate seasonal management of these, legal protection. and useful contacts for further help and advice. One leaflet is completely dedicated to *Greater Horseshoe Bats*. Dorset only has two confirmed breeding roosts for this rare bat which has declined significantly and is threatened with extinction. Another leaflet gives distribution maps of some of the commoner species in the county. The RSPB have also produced a useful leaflet about making a bat box which will help bats find new roosting sites if existing ones are damaged or destroyed.

May

Early entomologists coined the word aristocrats for the largest and most colourful of butterflies to be seen in this country, to which they gave splendid names such as *Purple Emperor, Painted Lady* and *Red Admiral.* Others include the *Peacock, Comma. White Admiral, Small Tortoiseshell* and the very rare *Large Tortoiseshell* and *Camberwell Beauty.* The majority of these aristocrats are able to live through the winter as hibernating butterflies but the *Red Admiral* and *Painted Lady* are usually unable to survive other than the mildest of winters. and mostly come to us from the Continent or North Africa each Year.

The caterpillars of the aristocrats may be split into two groups i.e. those that mainly feed on stinging nettles and those that eat the leaves of other plants. Those feeding on nettles include the *Peacock, Red Admiral, Comma, Small Tortoiseshell* and sometimes the *Painted Lady*. Stinging nettles not only provide food for the caterpillars but also provide protection and both grazing animals and predators will be deterred by the stinging quality of the plant.

Although the adult butterflies of each kind of nettle feeder differ a great deal, there are many similarities in the eggs, caterpillars and chrysalises of each species but there are differences however, in the way the eggs of each species are laid and how the young caterpillars colonize the nettles, which can help in identification The eggs of the *Small Tortoiseshell* and the *Peacock* are laid in clusters whilst the others lay their eggs singly. The caterpillars of these two species live in groups feeding on the new shoots at the top of the plant and protect themselves with a silken canopy. The other caterpillars are solitary creatures and protect themselves with individual silk tents in the case of *Commas* and *Painted Ladies,* whilst *Red Admirals* make leaf tents.

We are fortunate in this area to have access to fields and hedgerows which have lots of nettles growing freely to provide food for the caterpillars of these lovely creatures. Look out for the tell tale silken tents this summer to see how many you can identify. If you are unable to find any but would like to watch caterpillars grow and then turn into butterflies which can be released in the garden. you may be interested in a 'Butterfly Production Kit' which is available from Just Green. This consists of a special chamber containing five caterpillars. food plant and full instructions. Details from freephone 0800 389 6002 or visit the website www.just-green.com

A White Admiral Butterfly

*June*_____

On most mornings I walk my two Whippets along the Shave Cross Road to Blackmore Farm and back. Since the beginning of the year I have kept a record of the first sightings of any fauna or flora along this route and any adjoining fields. Although they might not be the very first sightings of specific species in the area this year, I thought that some of my records would be of interest to readers of these Nature Notes.

JANUARY

2nd -Primrose in flower outside Plenty House. Large flock **of** Herring Gulls flying North. I wondered where to.

5th -Two very large puffball mushrooms in field next to Peace Farm.

6th - Lungwort in bloom rear of our garden.

7th - Many more primroses in flower by Plenty House which suggest that the earlier one seen was not a sport.

9th -   Saw a Grey Squirrel using overhead telephone cable as a tightrope running from pole to pole.

12th-First daffodil in flower.

16th -. Rooks 'parliament' near Peace Farm.

17th -Tufted Vetch bloom seen. Probably a sport.

19 th - Snowdrops in flower by Hinkhams.

25th - Lesser Celandine in flower at the end of our garden.

30th - Chiff Chaff at the end of our garden. Is this evidence of some spending the winter here?

FEBRUARY

4th - Frogs in the old lake to east of Shave Cross Road.

6th - Five Canada Geese on the new lake to the east of the road.

14th - Several squashed toads on the road.

17th- Clumps of frogs' spawn in the old lake.

MARCH

3rd - Pair of Herons on the new lake. Were they a breeding pair? Where is the nearest heronry?

4th - Wild Daffodils in flower.

8th - Evidence of Rooks and Starlings nesting.

16th- Ladies Smock in flower.

18th - Blackthorn blooming.

19th - Isolated blooms of Greater Stitchwort and Red Campion.

21st - Peacock butterfly end of our garden.

22nd-Coltsfoot in flower.

25th -Toad's spawn and new Frog's in new lake. Marsh Marigold blooming.

30th -Pair of Canada Geese on new lake. Are they a breeding pair?

3lst -Sported nests of the following birds in the sparsely leaved hedgerows :- Hedge Sparrow, Song Thrush, Wren and Chaffinch. Being easily visible to me I suspect that some will fall victim to predators.

Primrose Flowers

In March there was an article in *The Independent* on a new book about Bumblebees in the UK which I thought might be of interest to readers of these 'Nature Notes'.

After butterflies *Bumblebees* are probably Britain's most popular insects. Everybody seems to like them. They are boldly coloured, they appear cuddly in a hairy kind of way-although with their sting you wouldn't want to cuddle them-they are hard-working, and they are an inveterate sign of Spring. We like the sight of them, we like their drowsy buzzing, and we feel they don't have the menace of their relations, the *Wasps*. Yet although many people could name and identify at least half a dozen of our butterfly species, not one in 10,000 could do the same for any of the 21 types of *Bumblebees* that inhabit our island. Who for example, can tell the difference between the *Garden Bumblebee* and the *Buff-tailed Bumblebee*? I must confess that I couldn't.

This might start to change however, with the publication of the first comprehensive photographic guide to *British Bumblebees*. Entitled' Field Guide to Bumblebees of Great Britain and Ireland' and published by Ocelli it costs £9.99 plus £1.25 postage and packaging. It can be obtained through book stores or www.ocelli.co.uk. This book offers a brightly original way of separating the different species, instead of the usual method employed by entomologists for identification i.e. killing them and putting them under the microscope. It displays a colour chart showing the different colour bands on the bee's thorax(its front half) and its abdomen. When used with adjoining charts showing the head shape of each species, its typical habitat and the time of year it appears - not to mention remarkable photographs by Ted Benton - it offers the best way yet to identify them in the flower beds.

The most important reason for doing so, say the authors , the bee experts Mike Edwards and Martin Jenner, is because British *Bumblebee* species are declining. Over the past two decades populations of some of the rarer species have seriously declined, and even the commoner ones are not as numerous as they were. This has given cause for alarm as they are important pollinators of wild and garden flowers, fruit trees and some crops. *Bumblebee* populations have declined for a number of reasons and we need to know more about these fascinating insects.

Bumblebees form a separate genus. or group of bees, with some forming a specialist sub-group known as *Cuckoo Bumblebees*, which take over the nests of other species. They are different from the *Honeybee* which produces large amounts of honey for its colony. *Bumblebees* produce only a small amount when a colony is founded by a queen

A Bumble Bee Collecting Nectar

August

Before I moved from London to Dorset I had little interest in wild flowers. I had some vague childhood memories about daisy chains and reflecting buttercups to determine whether I liked butter, but apart from that, wild flowers were a complete mystery to me. When I came to Whitchurch, all this changed. The local hedgerow verges were full of all kinds of flowering plants in every season of the year and I was mesmerized by this and wanted to know what each flower was called. One way of identifying them I thought might be to take photographs of the individual flowers in close-up and then identify them in a suitable handbook. This was easier said than done. There are possibly scores of different wild flowers to be seen in the Marshwood Vale throughout the year and it was not possible to photograph all of these so I decided that I would concentrate on the more numerous varieties. This approach has worked well and I am now familiar with most of the common wild flowers to be seen locally. The camera I used first of all was the one that I took my close-up butterfly pictures on i.e. the old manual single reflex camera with an extension ring and a fairly primitive flashgun. Things have now moved on in terms of automatic functioning and I went along with this firstly to a new up to date single lens reflex camera and recently a digital one. The digital camera has many advantages over the others in that it can focus down to one centimetre from a flower and it is possible to see the results immediately and to correct every image on the computer before printing it.

Going through the year the first hedgerow wild flowers usually to be seen are snowdrops. In February these are followed by the yellow flowed primroses, coltsfoot and lesser celandine. In March and April there is a profusion of the white blossoms of greater stitchwort, wild garlic and garlic mustard. In parts of Dorset April is the month to see large areas covered with cowslips but locally I have only seen them in small numbers. June brings forth the tricolour of white oxeye daisies and cow parsley, the blue of bluebells and the dark pink of red campion and foxgloves. Later in the year the blues of knapweed, tufted vetch and various thistles predominate inter-dispersed with the white fluffy beards of meadowsweet. Come late summer the yellows return in the form of fleabane and ragwort. Hedgerow verges are usually trimmed in early July and it may be mid August before they have a new flush of wild flowers. Some verges are set aside and not cut however because of their special wild flower interest. They are usually marked in Dorset by blue painted posts at the beginning and end of each protected verge. On these sites there are lots of different species to be seen all throughout the Summer. Before the introduction of specific herbicides most meadows also would have had a marvellous display of wild flowers before they were cut for hay. Poppies, corn cockles, snakehead fritillaries, ragged robin, meadow buttercup, bugle and various thistles. The list is endless. There are still a few meadows in the Vale that still have a good display of these plants but the majority just have a single type of grass growing. Things might be changing however as more land is being set aside to support wildlife. Certainly the areas where wild flowers are given a free reign are growing in the Vale. It is very difficult to commit to paper the joy these wild flowers arouse. They have obviously been a source of inspiration to many poets, writers and artists. In Dorset Thomas Hardy has described them in his novels and William Barnes in his local dialect poems. For me they have added an extra dimension to my appreciation of the natural world.

Garlic Mustard Blossom

September

On several days in Spring and Summer I visit Portland with a view to seeing a number of species of butterflies that don't normally occur locally in any numbers and, if possible, photographing them. Usually I go to some of the old quarries in the north of the island and to the butterfly reserve at Easton. Portland is the home to many of the butterflies whose caterpillars' food plants grow on the limestone that abounds on the island. It also has an abundance of nectar plants for the adult insects.

My first visits are made in May when I hope to make sightings of *Dingy Skippers, Grizzled Skippers, Adonis Blues* and *Brown Argus*. The food plants for the caterpillars of the former are Bird's-foot Trefoil and Horseshoe Vetch. The caterpillars of the *Grizzled Skipper* feed mainly on Wild Strawberry, those of the *Adonis Blue* on Horseshoe Vetch and those of the *Brown Argus* on Rockrose. The later species is a member of the Blue Family and their caterpillars, like many of their cousins are tended by ants. In June I look for *Common Blues* and *Small Blues*. The former occur in large numbers on Portland where their caterpillars feed on Birds- foot Trefoil and Black Medic. There is a second brood in August. The *Small Blue* is our smallest butterfly and is not as numerous as the *Common Blue*. It lays its eggs on Kidney Vetch.

. July is the month that I look for the magnificent *Dark Green Frittillary*. The numbers of this butterfly have decreased greatly and I am lucky to spot one or two specimens each year. Local older people confirm this decline. The eggs of this butterfly are laid on the leaves of Dog Violet and the caterpillars eat their eggshells after hatching then immediately they go into hibernation. In the following March they begin to feed on violet leaves until they pupate in June. The butterflies hatch a month later and live for about six weeks. Another July butterfly is the *Silver Studded Blue* a scarce blue butterfly that can be confused with the *Common Blue*. The caterpillars of this butterfly use a large range of food plants including Gorse, Heathers, Ling, Bird's-foot Trefoil and Rockrose. These caterpillars are attractive to ants who milk them for a sweet secretion they produce and when they pupate they are often buried in ant cells where they are protected from predators.

The August butterflies include second broods of *Common Blues, Adonis Blues* and the *Brown Argus*. The first sightings of the *Chalkhill Blue* occur this month. The males are powder blue in colour to attract females and the females are a drab brown to conceal them from predators. Their caterpillars feed on Horseshoe Vetch, and, like those of *Silver Studded Blues*,are protected by ants who in return gain by milking them of a sweet fluid they secrete. Other butterflies which may be seen on the island at this time include *Small Coppers, Graylings, Holly Blues, Walls* and, in some years, *Painted Ladies* and *Clouded Yellows*.

A Male Small Blue Butterfly

December

The only time that I saw a live *Hedgehog* in Dorset was on the very day that Doreen and I moved into Trumps In Cottage nearly twenty years ago. After a traumatic journey from our old London house we arrived in Whitchurch well after dark and ahead of the removal van that contained our furniture. We were very depressed by the prospect of spending the night in an empty cottage without any curtains, carpets and bedding etc. but our spirits were lifted by seeing a hedgehog shuffling about in the garden outside. Shortly afterwards our bedding did arrive and we settled down for the night. Since then I have only seen dead hedgehogs at the side of roads and lanes obviously killed by passing traffic, and the number of these sightings have declined over the years. 'Where have they all gone? Have any readers of these Nature Notes seen live or dead *Hedgehogs* lately?

Recently the *Hedgehog* was voted Britain's favourite garden animal in a survey of garden wildlife organised by the Royal Horticultural Society and The Wildlife Trusts.. It came ahead of the *Robin*, the *Frog*, the *Blackbird* and the *Ladybird*. Why should this be. Looking at hedgehog 1ore, it would seem that we tend to regard them as attractive, helpful and perhaps most of all, curiously vulnerable in a way that catches our sympathy. *Hedgehogs* are clearly still welcome in our gardens whereas *Squirrels. Moles, Foxes, Rabbits* and *Deer* are not. The secret of their attraction is perhaps that they are so visibly different. Britain's only spiny mammal, with its ability to curl up in a defensive ball of spikes, a living wonder in its way that cannot be mistaken for anything else. Its strategy of rolling into a ball to protect itself from danger seems to work most of the time. A *Stoat* or *Fox* cannot get the ball opened. This rolling up technique is useless however when a *Badger* comes along because badgers have such strong front paws that they can actually unroll the rolled up spiny ball. It is also useless when it is run over by a car.

Are these two factors the reasons why these lovely animals are not as common as they once were or is there some other reason for their decline? Slug pellets are often quoted as a cause of the decrease in the numbers of this animal but no scientific evidence appears to have been produced to support this theory. Are the locally increased number of *Badgers* in this area responsible for the dearth of *Hedgehogs* that can be seen here or is there some other explanation? Recent information from the Royal Botanic Gardens at Kew, where 300 acres of leafy landscape make absolutely perfect territory for these animals, there is not a single *Hedgehog* to be seen. Why? Because the *Badgers* at Kew have eaten every last one of them! So is this what has happened here? If it is the case then it is sad because many people are also very fond of *Badgers*. I am one of those people but I must say that their numbers appear to have increased lately and they now seem to create as much damage in gardens as *Moles* and *Deer*.

A Selection of Nature Notes Published in 2006

May

  In the very first Nature Notes I wrote that the wild flowers that grow in and around Whitchurch seem to be making their first appearances earlier and earlier each year. *Snowdrops* at the beginning of January and *Primroses* not much later. These were followed by *Lesser Celandine* and *Colts-foot* in mid February with *Greater Stichwort*, *Lungwort* and *Lady's Smock* appearing in early March. There were also early appearances of many of our fauna. Clumps of *Frogs Spawn* appeared in my garden pond in early January and *Brimstone*, *Peacock* and *Small Tortoiseshell* butterflies were on the wing at the very beginning of March. A possible reason for these early appearances was put down to Global Warming and I suggested that if the trend continued we might see some really spectacular early appearances and also that some species who are normally native to warmer climes might put in an appearance.

. Most winters since then have indeed been mild and the earlier trends have continued. However, what an exception this winter has been! Very cold and dry weather continuing for many weeks. A few *Snowdrops* did appear on cue but everything else lagged behind. There were very few *Primroses* to be seen in flower before the middle of March and flowers on the *Lesser Celandine* did not make an appearance in any numbers until the end of that month. The other flowers mentioned above had not put in an appearance by the time I wrote these notes. Clumps of Frogs Spawn were not apparent in local ponds until the third week of March and no butterflies have been spotted in my garden since last October. The last winter to be as cold as this was in 1986/87 shortly after I moved here. At that time I saw quite a few birds in the garden that had flown here to escape extremely cold weather and lack of food further north e.g. Fieldfare and Redwing. Such species did not seem to appear last winter. A few unusual native species were spotted in the village however looking for food. These included a female Blackcap and a possible Woodcock.

It will be interesting to see whether this late spring is a one off which will eventually catch up with previous ones in respect of the appearance of our individual fauna and flora. However, April is a fickle month in terms of weather. A recent article in the national press pointed out that there was no doubt that in the past twenty years warm sunny weather has been more common in April than in the 1960s and 1970s. April temperatures then averaged 8C and sunshine 127 hours. In the 1990s the equivalent figures were 8.4C and 150 hours. As I suggested in the first Nature Notes this might be due to the warming trend in the world's climate. Records of mean temperature and hours of sunshine made in the1940s however, showa mean temperature of 8.5C and 167 hours of sunshine. These figures suggest that there might be a cycle of warmer and cooler springs that are independent of any global warming. Personally I feel that the effects of global warming are now very apparent but that possibly there are some cyclical factors at work as well.

During the cold weather I put out plenty of food for our feathered friends. For the last month we have been visited every day by a *Long - Tailed Tit* who incessantly knocks at our window with his beak and flutters his wings like a fledgeling. Why does he do this? Does he see his reflection in the glass and try to make contact with it? Does he not see the glass and wants to fly into the cottage or is there some other reason? Perhaps some readers have experienced similar occurrences with other birds.

June

Our friendly *Long Tailed Tit* keeps knocking at our window but I am still unable to solve the mystery of why it does it. Originally there were two birds feeding simultaneously from the bird food containers that I had put up outside our main window at the front of the cottage, but now only one at a time appears. Perhaps there are a pair of these splendid birds but only one at a time comes to eat from our feeders because they have a nest nearby. If this is the case I have been unable to spot where it is.

Despite the cold weather in March and early April many of our resident birds seemed to have started nesting at the same time as in previous years. The local hedgerows, where many local birds build their nests, did not come into leaf this year until much later than usual and it was easy to see many nests that in other years would have been hidden by leaves. My main concern about this situation was that if I could see these nests easily then sharp eyed predators could spot them even more so. This did not seem to be the case however. Eggs hatched in all the nests that I had spotted and in nearly every case the chicks successfully fledged.

No local frogs appeared in my pond this year so I had to ask a neighbour if she could let me have some frogs' spawn from her pond. She was able to let me have three clumps two of which I put in opposite ends of my pond and the other in a ten litre bucket which I had filled with pond water. The spawn in the pond did hatch but the tiny tadpoles disappeared within a few days and I have been unable to ascertain why. The spawn in the bucket also hatched and in that case the tadpoles survived. In order to keep the water in the bucket at the same level as that in the pond I stood it on one of the marginal levels so that the pond water came up to its neck. As the tadpoles in the bucket grew larger I gradually released some of them into the pond where they seem to be flourishing. If these tadpoles safely turn into baby frogs I will repeat the experiment next year but use more buckets.

Readers may wish to know that our wonderful churchyard of St Candida and the Holy Cross has been entered into the Living

Churchyard Project, 2006 Competition run by Dorset Wildlife Trust in conjunction with the Diocese. It is expected that the judges will visit us in June on a date that will be notified. The wildflowers in the churchyard have been spectacular so far this year with a huge swathe of *Snowdrops* followed by *Primroses, Lesser Celandine* and *Ladies Smock*.. More nesting boxes have been put up recently in the churchyard and at least one was occupied within days. In last year's competition we were Very Highly Commended (good, but a step down from the 2004 award of Best Newcomer) One issue, commented on adversely by the judges last year, is seeing if we can keep mowings, clipping and spoil in a more orderly and sightly way- which would benefit wildlife and make the churchyard look better. It is hoped that these areas will be improved this year.

If anyone would like more information about the local Living Churchyard Group, or would like to join, please have a word with Barry Welch on 01297- 489116.

Long Tailed Tits

July_____

In my younger days, listening to bird song was one of the great delights of spring and early summer. Over the years however, my hearing gradually got weaker and weaker and it became increasingly difficult to appreciate this wonderful phenomenon. An old analogue hearing aid provided by the NHS did little to improve matters but recently they provided me with two digital hearing aids, one for each ear. What a difference these have made! I can now hear bird song more clearly than at any time that I can remember. Magic!

What I did not know however is why do birds sing and so I have been reading up on this. According to some ornithologists song is only one aspect of a bird's vocabulary. Each kind of bird makes a number of other calls too. There are alarm calls, aggressive calls and courtship calls. It seems difficult for naturalists to say exactly what is a song and what is a call. Song seems to be concerned mainly with defending a territory or attracting a mate. Calls however are made to pass on other information e.g. alerting other birds to the presence of a predator. Most birds that sing can be distinguished by one and another by their songs and thereby their species. This species identification by song helps prevent cross-breeding between similar looking birds e.g. a *Willow Warbler* and a *Chiffchaff*. At the same time, a bird's song is a statement of its sex which in most cases is male. Such songs are interpreted according to the sex of the hearer i.e. attracting females but repelling intruding males. These may not be all the reasons why birds sing and in fact some ornithologists no longer dismiss the idea that some birds may do so purely from high spirits. Listening to some of the splendid birds singing in my garden seems to reinforce this idea.

To help me identify some of the bird songs I recently invested in a DVD ROM to use on my computer called 'A Concise Guide to British Birds.' This covers 120 of the commonest birds that occur in the UK. It has over 250 video clips of these birds and over 250 songs and calls. It really is a splendid guide. It is published by BIRDGUIDES, Jack House, Ewden, Sheffield,S36 4ZA. My copy was purchased at the RSPB Centre at Radipole Lake in Weymouth. I can really recommend this guide to all my readers who want to extend their knowledge of British birds.

September

One of the joys of my childhood was going on holiday to the seaside where I was able to spend a lot of my time discovering seashells. Even in the war years I managed to get to the coast whilst evacuated to safer parts of the country and continued this passion. By the end of the war I had amassed quite a collection of the seashells that could be found around the English coasts. These were eventually passed on to younger children as I entered my teens and got interested in many other things. The interest returned however, when I took up pottery and looked for inspiration in natural things to design and glaze my pots. The seashells I then collected came from the four corners of the world and were of many shapes, sizes and finishes. They have had quite an influence on my pottery over the years.

Seashells are made by the group of creatures known as *Molluscs*. These include *Clams, Conches, Oysters, Periwinkles, Scallops* and *Whelks*. They form the second largest group, next to the insects, in the animal kingdom with over 60,000 known living species. Not all however have shells e.g. *Slugs* and many *Squids*. Those that do have them, particularly seashells, are divided into two groups; the *Gastropods* that have a single shell and the *Bivalves* that have two interlocking ones. Molluscs differ from other invertebrates in that they have two unique organs not found elsewhere. One of these is the **mantle**, a fleshy cape-like organ that surrounds the cavity where the gills, anus and kidney exit. The other is the **radula**, which is a long, tongue-like organ bearing many sharp hook-like teeth. The mantle has many microscopic glands that produce the shell of the individual creature from the calcium carbonate these glands exude. Colouration of the shell material comes from the pigments produced by special glands embedded in the edge of the mantle. Bands, zigzag lines and triangles are produced by the migration and sporadic production of pigments by these special glands. The diet of a mollusc can also have an effect on the extent of any colouration.

In Victorian times a great number of collections of shells were built up in this country. Shells were also used to decorate buildings and for Arts and Crafts projects. The most sought after marine shells were those belonging to the *Cone Family* all of which have a basic simple design of a cone with really wonderful and varied designs on them.

A Cone Shell

November

This year has been a splendid one for sightings of many different butterflies and moths, both locally and in Dorset as a whole.

1. BUTTERFLIES:-
Starting in March I saw various species of butterfly nectaring from the purple flowers of Honesty in my garden. Starting with *Brimstones* these were quickly followed by *Peacocks, Commas, Small Tortoiseshells, Red Admirals* and *Painted Ladies* . The first three would have probably hibernated over the winter but the latter two surprised me as they are normally thought not to be able to survive our cold winter climate. *Orange Tips* and *Green Veined Whites* appeared in early April and they also fed on the continuing Honesty flowers and on the white and pink Valerian flowers which had just come into bloom in my garden. Later some *Holly Blues* also joined in the feast together with a number of *Speckled Woods*. June saw the early arrival of a few *Meadow Browns, Ringlets* and *Marbled Whites* in the meadows around Whitchurch although only the *Meadow Browns* actually appeared in my garden to drink nectar from golden Globe Buddleia flowers that were in bloom. All of these butterflies presented many opportunities to photograph them! The highlights of the year in my garden however must be the spotting of a *Silver Washed Fritillary* on my purple buddleia bush in July and later some *Small Coppers* feeding on Michaelmas daisies. Both firsts for me.

Further afield in the county there were also some spectacular sightings. Powerstock Common in July was populated by unusually large numbers of *Silver Washed Fritillaries* and *Marbled Whites* and the quarries on Portland were frequented by a large number of *Clouded Yellows, Adonis Blues, Silver Studded Blues* and *Chalkhill Blues*. The most exciting recorded sightings in the county however were of a *Monarch Butterfly* in a garden near Sherborne and two *Camberwell Beauties*, one in Charminster, the other in Higher Woodford. Monarch butterflies are natives of North America and each year migrate in huge numbers from the United States and Canada to winter in Mexico. They are occasionally brought to this country by very strong westerly winds and most often found in the Scilly Isles and Cornwall. Camberwell Beauties however come from Eastern Europe and this year more than 100 were seen in East Anglia.

2. MOTHS

Moth sightings this year seem even more spectacular than those of the butterflies. In my garden there were almost daily visits by *Humming bird Hawk -moths* during the summer, sipping nectar from Valerian flowers or White Agastarche. This day-flying species, which was formally a rare summer visitor from Southern Europe, is now thought to be resident here and a British breeding species. The food plants for its caterpillars are Bedstraw and Wild Madder. Large numbers of another day- flying moth the *Silver Y* appeared in July. It comes from North Africa and its numbers seem to increase each year.

When visiting Powerstock Common in July I saw a large number of *Scarlet Tiger* moths flying with the butterflies there . These beautiful moths tend to form localized colonies and to find one such colony was another first for me. In early September a neighbour telephone to say that a number of *Convolvulus Hawk-moths* were visiting the Nicotiana plants in his garden at dusk seeking out their nectar. Before I could get up to his garden however the weather changed and they did not appear again! But later I was shown a corpse of one of the moths which confirmed its identity. This is our second largest moth another immigrant from the Mediterranean which also seems to be visiting us more frequently. An interesting factor about this species is that it has an incredibly long proboscis, up to 90mm long which, when not in use, is coiled up underneath its body. I would have loved seeing this in use! Hopefully more will come next year.

A Scarlet Tiger Moth

A Selection of Nature Notes Published in 2007

January

Our local deciduous trees seem to have hung on to their leaves later than usual this year and there has been a good display of autumnal colours throughout November.

Why do deciduous trees shed their leaves each year? One theory is that they do this because they cannot get enough water from frozen or very cold soil to maintain transpiration i.e the loss of water vapour from the surface of a tree, which occurs primarily through the small pores in the leaves. Was our very hot summer followed by heavy rains responsible for the late leaf shedding this year? What caused the autumnal colours before the leaves finally fell? Such colouring normally occurs because the green chlorophyll breaks down as the leaves fade and pigments called *carotenes* become visible as shades of yellow, orange and scarlet.

When I was a child I learnt to recognize many of our broad leaf deciduous trees by their leaves. I kept a collection of such leaves by drying them in an improvised flower press which consisted of sheets of old newspapers weighed down by a very heavy book. This collection also included the skeletons of leaves that were left after the fleshy parts had decayed. The shapes of these leaves fell into the following classes:-

    a) **Simple Undivided**. These were oval in shape with veins that spread out from the base or branch out from a central vein e.g. the leaves of some *Cherry Trees* *b)* **Palmately Lobed**. Leaf blades have three, five or seven lobes with main veins that run out at angles from the leaf stalk e.g. *Fig Leaves*

c) **Palmately Compound**. Leaves that have separate divided leaflets which radiate from the main stalk e.g. leaves on a *Horse Chestnut Tree*

d) **Pinnately Lobed**. The leaf blade has a number of lobes projecting from either side, each lobe having veins that run out from the central mid rib e.g. leaves of various *Oak Trees*

e) **Pinnately Compound**. These leaves bear from five to twenty leaflets e.g. *Mountain Ash Leaves*

The shapes and veins of various leaves were an inspiration to me when I studied pottery. They could be used as stencils, pressed into the surface of soft clay or used as an underglaze covering before a pot was finally fired. One of my favorite uses was to impress the underneath of a leaf into soft clay and when it it hardened I would rub copper oxide into the impression which , when fired, would leave a metallic green design showing through the glaze. Magic stuff!

A Fig Leaf

May

In my Nature Notes for May 2002 I mentioned that I had missed hearing the Cuckoo's song that year and put forward a number suggestions for this. The main one was that because of *Global Warming* the caterpillars that formed the Cuckoo's favorite food were not available because the leaves on which they fed were too tough to eat when they hatched out. This may be part of the reason that they were not heard then. Five years later, and despite being fitted with high tech. digital hearing aids, I have still not heard one.

A recent article in the Independent Newspaper suggested that the Cuckoo, one of our favourite birds, may be in terminal decline. For such a familiar bird to be in such trouble is extremely worrying. In fact according to the Royal Society for the Protection of Birds such is the crisis in Cuckoo numbers that it is expected that the cuckoo will soon be added to the Red List, a register of the UK,s most threatened breeding birds. So what is causing them to decrease so alarmingly? The Independent's investigation into this came up with a number of possible reasons. Cuckoos lay their eggs in the nests of other birds and get them to raise their young.

One factor is thought to be the decline of the Cuckoo's key host species. Although some fifty of them are chosen as possible foster parents just three species make up 80 per cent of these. They are the Dunnock, Meadow Pipit and Reed Warbler. However, the number of Meadow Pipits have fallen by 40 per cent over the past 30 years. Similarly the number of Dunnocks are down by 40 per cent. No figures were given for any possible decline in the number of Reed Warblers nesting here.

Another possible factor for the decrease in the number of Cuckoos breeding here is the fall in the number of moths found in the UK whose caterpillars are a major source of food for them. The large hairy caterpillars of the Garden Tiger Moth are poisonous to all British birds apart from the Cuckoo and the numbers of this moth have also decreased by 40 per cent over the past 30 years.

The main reason for the decline in numbers of this bird however is thought to be in East Africa where they overwinter. This area is increasingly being hit by drought as a result of *Climate Change* which is making conditions there more difficult for wild life. Other bird species such as Sand Martins and Sedge Warblers are experiencing a similar decline in numbers.

Climate Change now seems a reality and the Cuckoo is one of its victims. Sadly it seems that we can no longer count on it as the harbinger of Spring!

July

In nature one of the commonest ways plants and trees reproduce themselves is by producing seeds that contain the genes of the parent plants. These seeds are formed after pollen, which is manufactured by the anthers of a flower, is deposited on the stigma of a flower thus fertilizing the ovary. This may happen within the same flower or the pollen may come from another of the same or similar species. This transfer of pollen is usually done by insects, often bees, collecting nectar that is produced by that flower. After fertilization the seeds produced in the ovary ripen and are then dispersed.

Plants and trees disperse their seeds in many ways, each species having its own particular method which ensures that each seed has the best chance of germinating and growing. These methods include seeds that:-

1) ripen inside fruits and berries and are dispersed in the droppings of birds and animals that eat them e.g. *Blackberries, Elderberries,* the fruits of *Hawthorn, Holly, Rowan, Bilberry, Buckthorn Trees* and *Rose Hips*

2) are stored by animals for winter use but remain uneaten. Examples are various *Acorns, Beechnuts, Cobnuts* and *Sweet Chestnuts*

3) are dispersed by the wind by:-

a) having a gossamer Parashoot. These include *Dandelion, Goats Beard, Willowherb,* several *Thistles, Cudweed, Colts-foot and Valerian,*

b) having wings eg *Ash, Sycamore, Maple, Elm, Hornbeam, Silver Birch* and *Tree of Heaven* seeds

4) are spread by exploding pods such as *Himalayan Balsam,* several *Vetches, Gorse, Herb Robert* and *Cranesbill*

5) that have hooks or barbs that get caught on the fur or feathers of passing animals and birds and which drop off later. These are found on such plants as *Wild Carrots, Avens, Agrimony, Burdock, Goose Grass* and *Nodding Bur Marigold*

All these methods ensure that young plants do not grow up in the shade of their parents and allows them to colonize pastures new.

Photograph by Barry Welch

Winged Dandelion Seeds

September

The Marine Conservation Society (MCS) are holding a survey of the *Jellyfish* that occur around our coasts. This is part of a study into how to protect the critically endangered leather back turtles that migrate thousands of miles to UK waters to feed on their favourite jellyfish prey.

Jellyfish are not in fact fish, but a class of invertebrates called the *Scyphozoans*. They start out in life as simple polyps attached to rocks but then develop into a floating medusa, with a radially-symmetrical umbrella shaped body called a bell. These creatures have a simple body plan and are just one step removed from colonies of individual animals clumped together. They possess tentacles armed with batteries of stinging cells. Each of these cells has a stinging apparatus called a nematocyst which is essentially a sac of poison attached to a sharp, hollow tube armed with barbs. The stinging cell works like a jack-in-the-box springing out when brushed by a passing arm or leg. Being stung by just one nematocyst would probably not be felt but having thousands injecting their toxin could be very painful or even dangerous. There are about 10,000 species around the world and more than 100 are toxic to humans.

For the purpose of their survey MCS are only interested in the larger jellyfish that might be seen in our coastal waters and give the following details in their identification guide:-

COMPASS JELLYFISH. This is typically up to 30cm in diameter. Colour is variable but usually has a pale umbrella shaped bell with diagnostic brownish V shaped markings, 32 marginal lobes, 24 long tentacles and 4 frilled thick arms. **This jellyfish stings**.

MOON JELLYFISH. This transparent jellyfish has an umbrella-shaped bell edged with short hair-like tentacles which can grow up to 40cm in length. Its sting is mild and the most distinguishing feature is the four purple rings in the centre of its bell.

MAUVE STINGER. This jellyfish can reach up to 10cm in diameter and has a deep bell with pink or mauve warts. It has 16 marginal lobes, 8 marginal hair-like tentacles and 4 longer frilled arms with small pink spots. **This jellyfish Stings.**

LION'S MANE JELLYFISH. Grows to 50cm but can grow to 2 metres in diameter. It has a large reddish brown umbrella shaped with a mass of long, thin, hair-like tentacles in addition to four short, thick frilled and folded arms. **This jellyfish stings.**

BLUE JELLYFISH Similar in shape to the preceding species but is smaller with a blue bell through which radial lines can be seen. It's sting is mild.

BY -THE –WIND- SAILOR Not a true jellyfish but a floating colony of individual creatures known as a *hydranth*. Occur in large swarms.

BARREL OR ROOT MOUTH JELLYFISH This is a robust creature that grows up to 1M in diameter. It has a largely white bell fringed with purple. The bell lacks tentacles but has 8 thick frilled arms hanging below.

PORTUGUESE MAN-OF-WAR This is not a true jellyfish but a floating colony of microscopic *hydrozoans*. Its distinguishing feature is the oval float complete with crest below which hang many fishing polyps that can be up to 10M long. It is rare in UK waters but sometimes turns up in the South West.
It's sting is very dangerous and if seen in any numbers should be reported to the local authorities

Details of the survey can be seen on www.mcsuk.org where the jellyfish identification chart and survey forms can be downloaded. Alternatively they can be obtained from MSC, Unit 3, Wolf Business Park, Alton Road, Ross-on-Wye, HR3 5NB

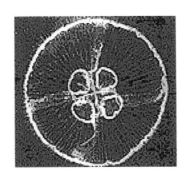

A Moon Jellyfish

December

In previous Nature Notes I have explored the question of how Nature has influenced artists in the past. One of such artists is the poet John Clare and I quote below two of his splendid poems about birds one that is still a common bird and the other that was common in my childhood days but is now rarely seen:-

1. The Wren

Why is the cuckoos melody preferred
And nightingale's rich song so fondly praised
In poets' rhymes? Is there no other bird
Of nature's minstrelsy that oft hath raised
Ones heart to ecstasy and mirth as well?
I judge not how another's taste is caught;
With mine there's other birds that bear the bell
Whose song hath crowds of happy memories brought.
Such the wood Robin singing in the dell
And little Wren that many a time hath sought
Shelter from showers in huts where I did dwell
In early Spring, the tenant of the plain.
Tenting my sheep. and still they come to tell
The happy stories of the past again.

2 The Skylark

The rolls and harrows lie at rest beside
The battered road and, spreading far and wide
Above the russet clods, the corn is seen
Sprouting its spiry points of tender green.
Where squats the hare to terrors wide awake
Like some brown clod the harrows failed to break,
While neath the warm hedge boys stray far from home
To crop the early blossoms as they come;
Where buttercups will make them eager run
Opening their golden caskets to the sun
To see who shall be first to pluck the prize;
And from their hurry up the skylark flies
And o'er her half-formed nest with happy wings
Winnows the air — till in the clouds she sings,
Then hangs a dust spot in the sunny skies
And drops and drops till in her nest she Lies
Where boys unheeding passed — ne'er dreaming then
That birds which flew so high — would drop again
To nests upon the ground where any thing
May come at to destroy. Had they the wing
Like such a bird, themselves would be too proud
And build on nothing but a passing cloud,
As free from danger as the heavens are free
From pain and toil — there would they build and be
And sail about the world to scenes unheard
Of and unseen — oh were they but a bird.
So think they while they listen to its song
And smile and fancy and so pass along
While its low nest moist with the dews of morn
Lie safely with the leveret in the corn.

A Selection of Nature Notes Published in 2008

February

After what is said to have been our wettest summer since records began the effect on our wildlife needs to be assessed. Possibly the most affected will be birds and insects.

Because of the weather it has been suggested that birds that rely on insects to feed their young, have found such food in short supply. Consequently many chicks did not fledge thus depleting the number of adult birds that will breed next spring to a lower level than usual. What are the species that have been most affected? We will get some idea from the results of the 2008 Big Garden Bird Watch to be held on 19th January. In the meantime I have been keeping a not too accurate record of the species that have used my bird feeders in December and put the results up against those that used my feeders in the same period last year. This is not 'rocket science' but I thought that this would give some idea of what birds might have been affected. The results are given below.

BIRD SPECIES	NUMBERS SEEN
House Sparrow	more numerous than last year
Blue Tit	almost the same as last year
Great Tit	less numerous than last year
Coal Tit	much less numerous
Nuthatch	one seen both years
Robin	about the same as last year
Hedge Sparrow	about the same as last year
Green Finch	none seen, very common last year
Chaffinch	as for Green Finch
Gold Finch	none seen this year several last year
Long Tailed Tit	fewer than last year
Wren	none seen, few last year
Black Cap	one seen for the first time this year
Blackbird	about the same as last year

The lack of Green Finches and Chaffinches is worrying and could suggest that their numbers have indeed been depleted as a result of the wet summer. Alternatively it may be that these species did not like the food that I put out for them! It would be interesting to hear from readers of these Nature Notes whether these species had been spotted in their gardens

A Solitary Robin

March

In last month's Nature Notes I pondered whether the effect of last year's wet summer had affected our wild life especially as far as birds and insects were concerned. I speculated that some information about the effects of the heavy rainfall on our birds might be gleaned from the results of this year's Big Garden Birdwatch run by the RSPB in January.

The results of my own participation in this event were rather disappointing. Having decided that I might record a higher number of birds if I watched my bird feeders about an hour or so before dusk, when many birds fill up with food to sustain them overnight. How wrong I was! In total only nine birds showed up. These were:- 1 Blackbird, 2 Blue Tits, 1 Coal tit, 1 Dunnock, 1 Great Tit, 2 House Sparrows and 1 Robin. This was despite the fact that a group of Long Tailed Tits had put in an appearance just before I began my count. Sadly there was no sign of any Green Finches or Chaffinches the species I had been particularly worried about in my earlier article. In fact there has been no appearance of these species for some months now.

Feedback from a Reader in Morecombelake who does a weekly bird count for the British Trust for Ornithology suggested that the number of Green Finches and Chaffinches recorded by her in the last quarter of 2007 were less than usual. Another Reader also reported that she had seen fewer of these species in her garden recently. Other Readers of these Nature Notes who took part in the Big Garden Birdwatch may have had better results. We can only wait to receive the overall picture from the RSPB to see which species of birds have either declined or increased in numbers since the beginning of 2007.

Information about the effects of the wet summer on our insect population will probably have to wait until later this year, although already there are reports in the Press that the overall amount of honey produced by our Honey Bees last year is down by as much as 50%. I have no details of this and I wonder whether Bee Keepers in the Marshwood Vale have found this to be the case.

A Cock Sparrow

April

A recent item in the national press showed a photograph of a *Red Admiral* resting amongst Snowdrops in a Dorset churchyard. The article suggested that this was a sight that until a few years ago would have been impossible.

Until about 15 years ago Red Admirals were summer migrants to the UK but, with a warming climate and earlier springs, they have increasingly over-wintered in the southern counties. The picture was taken by Dr Martin Warren, chief executive of Butterfly Conservation, who says that this is real proof that climate warming is taking place. This species does not fully hibernate, but will be seen on any day that conditions are right. Well into November it can be seen refueling on late flowering plants such as Ivy and Michaelmas Daisies while also hanging drowsily about orchards where fallen fruit ferments temptingly on the ground. In mid winter oblivious to the calendar , it will take wing on any day warm enough to heat up its body. Its hunger for nectar will make it search out early blooming plants and trees. Hence its appearance in the delightfully named Turners Puddle churchyard on the Isle of Purbeck flitting from snowdrop to snowdrop was really magical.

Not surprisingly a Red Admiral was the first British butterfly spotted on New Year's Day in Kent. Other species seen on the wing in England up to the 8th February were a:-

Peacock in Leicestershire on 6th January
Brimstone in Wiltshire on 8th January
Painted Lady in Hampshire on 25th January
Small Tortoiseshell in Yorkshire on 25th January
Comma Sussex on 26th January
Speckled Wood Devon on 26th January

Small White Hants on 8th February

On Portland the Bird Observatory recorded a sighting of a *Peacock* on the 27th January.

I am happy to say that since last month's Nature Notes a pair of Green Finches have taken up residence in our garden. Sadly no Chaffinches have appeared.

A Peacock Butterfly

May

The results of the RSPB's **Big Garden Bird Watch** have now been published on the Internet.. The top10 birds in Dorset were:-

BIRD	AVERAGE NUMBER PER GARDEN
House Sparrow	3.37
Blackbird	2.62
Chaffinch	2.45
Blue Tit	2.29
Starling	2.01
Wood Pigeon	1.85
Green Finch	1.50
Robin	1.46
Great Tit	1.38
Gold Finch	1.22

Overall, the average number of birds seen in each garden in the UK has declined by a fifth since 2004, and House Sparrows have decreased by almost two thirds since 1979 and Starlings by three quarters over the same period. Despite this however the number of colourful finches visiting our gardens over this winter are at the highest levels for five years.

For the first time in the survey's 29 years history the striking Siskin made it into the top 20, and the scarce Brambling has moved up from 57 to 36 in the rankings. The increase in these species up by two thirds in the last five years suggests that tree seed supplies have been poor in 2007 and has forced them to come into gardens to find food. Along with Bramblings and Siskins Redpole numbers have rocketed, being seen in twice as many gardens as last year. Again this was probably due to poor tree seed supplies.

Gold Finch numbers however are probably the great success story of the survey. This wonderful finch has made it into the top 10 for the very first time. Gold Finch numbers have swelled because our milder winters have encouraged the to stay here instead of going to southern Europe. Our gardens can be very welcoming to these finches , especially those with Nyjer seed provided and, thistles and teasels left to grow which also provide food.

Before the Survey took place the RSPB thought that it would provide a picture of the impacts on common birds of rising temperatures, last year's wet summer and the increasing amount of food put out to attract birds. In particular they anticipated that there would be increases in the numbers of Gold Finches for the reasons given above, and decreases in the numbers of Blue Tits. In 2007 Blue Tits, which normally have only one brood a year, experienced their worst ever breeding season, with only just over a half of young Blue Tits fledging. May and July were the wettest months in England and Wales for over 200 years. Heavy rain washed caterpillars off of leaves and so the later emergence of caterpillars caused a food shortage for these birds.

The shortage of food however does not appear to have caused a problem for other birds such as Chaffinches and Green Finches as I speculated in an earlier Nature Notes! I must say however that I have still not seen a Chaffinch in my garden since last summer and only one pair of Green Finches. These species are still in the top ten recorded in our gardens. On the other hand Blue Tits have been the most frequent visitors to my feeders and I am personally surprised at the drop in their overall numbers as recorded in the survey.

A Gold Finch Feeding on Sunflower Kernels

June

The wild flower charity **Plantlife** runs Britains biggest annual wild plant survey. This survey is a long-term project monitoring changes to wild plants in the UK. Plantlife say that external factors are having an enormous impact on our environment and point out that in the five years since the survey started, they have already recorded significant changes in the countryside.

A new analysis of last year's survey suggests that even the commonest wild flowers are disappearing from the countryside in addition to many rarer species. This survey used volunteers to examine more than 500 sites across the country for the presence or absence of 65 different common or familiar plant species. The new analysis showed that of the 524 sites surveyed, 121 contained none of the 'common 65' whatsoever. Every county of England – except Co Durham- held sites that were completely empty of the target plants. The sites frequently holding nothing fell under the category 'arable and horticultural', which in essence means cornfields. Survey workers were looking for the presence of three flowers once regarded as absolutely cornfield plants- *scarlet pimpernel, common chickweed* and *common poppy*. Yet 52 out of the 107 cornfield plots in the survey contained no trace of any of them, indicating that something has gone very wrong, from a botanical point of view, with the arable plants in this country.

Another significant finding was the absence of common flowers in the category 'broadleaved woodland and scrub'. Here the number of sites holding nothing was smaller; six sites out of 81-but here the number of target species, i.e. 11 was much larger. They were:- *wood anemone, bluebell, herb robert, bugle, lords and ladies, red campion, lesser celandine, primrose, foxglove, golden saxifrage* and *traveller's joy*. This is in essence a litany of Britain's best loved and most familiar wild flowers, and to find a wood that contains none of them would be remarkable at any time; yet to find 7% of woods bare of foxgloves and absolutely everything else in the list shows that woodlands, like cornfields, are in botanical trouble. Further information about last year's survey and details about this years, including voluntary participation, can be obtained over the internet from www.plantlife.org.uk.

Despite the Plantlife surveys I must say that in the Marshwood Vale we are very fortunate in having a good display of many species of wild flowers on the wide verges and high banks of the many lanes in the area. Most of these are looked after by the West Dorset District Council who cut these areas at the best time to conserve the populations of the wild flowers from year to year. Areas which support many species of common plants, or are home to some rare ones, are marked out for special protection by a system of blue painted posts.

So far this year there have been some wonderful early displays locally of *snowdrops, primroses, lesser celandine,* and *ladies smock.* The latter species is probably my favourite as the flower has a unique colour not seen in other plants. On my morning walks along the Shave Cross Road, I encountered greater swathes of this flower which were much greater than I had seen in previous years. At the time of writing these Notes the lanes are bursting with a tricolour of red, white and blue. The red of *campion*, the white of *wild garlic, greater stitchwort* and *cow parsley,* and finally the wonderful colour of the native *bluebell.* Next will come the summer flowers and hopefully these will be just as splendid as in previous years.

A Wild Garlic Flower

November

Two wet summers in a row seem to have led to an explosion in the numbers of *slugs* and *snails* that can be seen in the garden so, I thought that I should do some research and devote this month's Nature Notes to them.

Sometimes referred to as soil animals these creatures are both **molluscs**, snails having a coiled shell and slugs having no shell or very little. Both crawl around on their muscular underside, which is called a foot, by means of wave ripples along the body which push them forward. They also produce slime which helps this operation. Slugs and most snails have two pairs of tentacles with eyes at the end of the larger ones. These eyes are very primitive and they are only able to see the difference between light and dark. The smaller tentacles are smelling organs and act as a nose. These creatures also have a small breathing hole on their side which opens and closes as they breathe. Most slugs and snails are hermaphroditic, ie both male and female. They still however need to mate with another of the same species. After mating each will lay up to a hundred eggs each hatching as a baby version of the parents. There are said to be up to 20 kinds of slugs and 80 kinds of snail that can be seen in this country.

The most common slugs to be found locally include:-

1) The *Grey Field Slug*
2) The *Large Black Slug*
3) The *Garden Slug*
4) Various species of *Keeled Slugs*

The most common snails are:-

1) The *Common Garden Snail*
2) Various *Banded Snails*

There are also a number of Pond Snails which were the subject of a previous Nature Notes about Garden Ponds

Apart from Gardeners slugs and snails have many enemies. These include Song Thrushes, the only bird that is able to break the shells of snails, Mistle Thrushes and Blackbirds who enjoy eating slugs but haven't learnt the trick of cracking snail shells. Slugs are also eaten by Hedgehogs, Frogs and Toads who prefer them to snails. Insects that eat slugs include Ground and Rove Beetles. The slime produced by slugs does however act as a deterrent against some of these predators.

A Garden Snail